UNDERSTANDING COUNTERTRANSFERENCE

From Projective Identification to Empathy

Michael J. Tansey
Walter F. Burke

UNDERSTANDING COUNTERTRANSFERENCE

From Projective Identification to Empathy

THE ANALYTIC PRESS

1989 Hillsdale, NJ Hove and London

Published by
The Analytic Press, Inc.
Editorial Offices: 101 West Street
Hillsdale, NJ 07642

Set in Melior type by TechType, Upper Saddle River, NJ

First paperback printing 1995

Library of Congress Cataloging-in-Publication Data

Tansey, Michael J.
Understanding countertransference.

Bibliography; p.
Includes index.
1. Countertransference I. Burke, Walter F. II. Title.
RC489.C68T36 1989 616.89'14 88-24217

ISBN 0-88163-227-9

Printed in the United States of America
10 9 8 7 6 5 4 3 2

To my parents, Connie and Walter
W. F. B.

To Pamela
M. J. T.

I had seen so many people all my life—I was an average mixer, but more than average in a tendency to identify myself, my ideas, my destiny, with those of all classes that I came in contact with. . . . I had become identified with the objects of horror or compassion . . . identification such as this spells the death of accomplishment. It is something like this that keeps insane people from working.

—F. Scott Fitzgerald, "The Crack Up," 1936

Contents

Preface

The inspiration for this work came predominantly from our association with Dr. Merton Gill. Having participated in his psychotherapy seminar during graduate school, we were fortunate enough to be able to form a weekly study group with him upon graduation. That group began in 1978, continues to meet, and has exerted a major impact upon clinical psychology throughout the city of Chicago. Unlike many others who have achieved eminence in this field, Merton has always encouraged independent thinking rather than conformity. He relishes spirited debate and is remarkably able to concede a point when the weight of clinical material calls for modifying his position. He has shown us by example that one need not expect perfection or omniscence from oneself, either as a teacher or as a therapist. Both by his words and—much more importantly—by his example, he established an attitude and tone within the study group that facilitated and encouraged the examination of often difficult countertransference experiences.

As we listened to audio-taped presentations of clinical material, a very common pattern caught our attention: because the study group was experienced as wonderfully helpful, each presenter typically brought in a difficult case, rather than one that would simply reflect his competency. Very often the difficulty revolved around some form of countertransference disturbance, producing such feelings as discomfort, self-doubt, and loss of perspective. With the group's insight and support, the therapist was frequently able to identify and acknowledge uncomfortable thoughts, feelings, and urges toward the patient. Time and again, it became clear that the disruptive countertransference response had in some way been brought on not only by the personal issues of the therapist, but also by the influence of the patient. Understanding the nature, source, and meanings of the patient's influence inevitably proved to be extremely valuable to the treatment process.

Because each therapist typically presented three or four times before we moved on to the next case, the group had the opportunity to test hypotheses by observing how the therapist chose to incorporate input from the group into his interventions, and how the patient subsequently responded. In addition, we often had the opportunity to hear the same case presented a year or two later. Consistently, we concluded that a greater understanding of the patient, the therapist, and the interaction evolved out of episodes of countertransference disturbance. Although the study group was organized out of a collective interest in Merton Gill's ideas regarding transference phenomena, we were inexorably led in the direction of understanding the therapist's experience as a vehicle for fathoming the patient's experience. We were then led quite naturally to a study of the literature pertaining to empathy, projective identification, and countertransference, the three most important concepts (along with transference) that bridge the intrapsychic and interpersonal realms.

We are profoundly grateful to Merton for all that he has done for us in fostering our professional growth over the years. We thank him for his encouragement and direction in the completion of this project. To the dozens of psychologists who have participated in this study group since inception, we also express our thanks.

From the study group, from our research of the literature, and from our cumulative clinical and supervisory experience, we came away with several questions that are addressed in this volume. How is the patient able to induce within the therapist those feeling states that so closely parallel or complement his own? What are the specific steps by which a therapist, struggling with countertransference, can extricate himself from the intensity of his experience, however pleasant or unpleasant it may be? Having extricated himself, how does he make use of the experience to further his understanding of the patient? How does he determine the extent of his own contribution to his countertransference response versus the extent of the patient's interpersonal influence? Lastly, how does the therapist decide on the content and timing of his interventions, which are grounded in understanding of his countertransference? When is countertransference disclosure useful and when is it not? We do not feel that these questions have been adequately addressed in the existing literature.

We were influenced and inspired too by Dr. Charles Donnelly, who died suddenly in 1987. His encouragement and his dedication to our professional development were strong factors in the early work leading up to this volume. His interest in understanding processes of internalization from the framework of ego psychology helped us to address the intrapsychic experience of the therapist caught in a countertransference storm. Above all, Charlie demonstrated an unwavering commitment to the application of psychoanalytic methods to severely disturbed patients. He thus helped to convince us that psychoanalytic concepts most often exist along a continuum and are not justifiably segregated according to indices of psychopathology.

For the variety of ways in which they assisted in the overall preparation of this book, we wish to thank Drs. Paula Gorlitz, Beth Carone, Norman Schaffer, Ronald Ganellen, Oliver Kerner, Craig Johnson, and Ted Stevens.

Lissa Pete's diligent efforts in typing and word processing the volume were nothing short of heroic. She was able to transform handwritten or hastily dictated material into comprehensible copy. Her dedication and resourcefulness quite literally made this publication possible.

Lastly, we are grateful to Eleanor Starke Kobrin for her editorial assistance in polishing the manuscript, and to Dr. Paul E. Stepansky, editor-in-chief of The Analytic Press, for his encouragement, patience, and reliability. We remain incredulous that he once responded in less than a week to five chapters of manuscript with three pages of detailed, thoughtful commentary.

UNDERSTANDING COUNTERTRANSFERENCE
From Projective Identification to Empathy

1 *Introduction*

The setting is a familiar one. Psychology and psychiatry residents, social work interns, postdoctoral fellows, and staff clinicians are seated in a circle for their monthly case conference. A tape recorder is present, and the resident whose work will be held up for scrutiny shifts nervously in his seat. At the designated time, the eagerly awaited consultant who is to discuss the case arrives promptly and moves to his chair, all eyes upon him. Small talk ceases as the invited guest is introduced.

The consultant asks a few brief questions: How old is the patient? How long and at what frequency has the patient been seen? What was the presenting complaint? Is there any particular problem with the case that the therapist wishes to be addressed? In the space of two or three minutes, these questions are answered by the therapist. Without further ado, the tape recorder is turned on and the audience listens attentively as a therapy session unfolds. Ten minutes into the session, the consultant leans over, pushes the stop button, smiles reassuringly at the presenting resident—who by this time is sweating bullets—and asks if anyone feels moved to comment on what has been heard.

There is a brief, uncomfortable silence. Finally, the boldest of the group ventures an observation about the patient's dynamics and triggers a flurry of similar brief remarks by others. But the discussion fades quickly away. The members have come to hear not from one another but from the consultant, whose moment has now arrived. He does not disappoint. Turning to face the presenting resident, he proceeds to deliver a series of well-articulated formulations about the nature of the current therapeutic interaction, its relationship to the genetic history of the patient, and some feelings with which the therapist might be struggling that had not yet been mentioned. The presenter nods vigorously on all counts, and the consultant—who is clearly having a good day—goes so far as to predict a shift in the direction of the material that might be coming within the very session under examination. The recording is turned back on, to the wide-eyed anticipation of all, and—voila!—the predicted shift irrefutably occurs. The hour strikes, the consultant rises and quickly departs, leaving behind a room filled with buzzing, bedazzled conversation.

Variations in the foregoing scenario are extremely common. The format may include audio tapes, process notes, case histories, one-way mirror observation, or live interviews. The audience may consist of trainees or even experienced clinicians. Such experiences for the participants are often tremendously energizing and inspirational, providing exposure to identificatory models who demonstrate the highest levels of clinical acumen. There is, however, frequently a problem that accompanies the sense of awe and mystification engendered by the seemingly dazzling ability of the gifted and experienced clinician. All too often, the audience is left to wonder just how these clever formulations and predictions were constructed. Therein lies a serious didactic gap in clinical training and preparation for which the therapist, especially the newly initiated, often comes to feel privately responsible.

It is undeniable that at the heart of any sophisticated formulation is the ability to be *empathic*. Indeed, the very term empathy has become the password of self psychology, representing an entire school of thought within the psychoanalytic spectrum. Kohut, the founder of the self-psychological movement, wrote the following widely quoted passage in a landmark paper on the subject (1959): "We speak of physical phenomena when the essential ingredient of our observational methods includes our senses, we speak of psychological phenomena when the essential ingredient of our observation is introspection and empathy" (p. 460).

What is this creature, empathy? Is it an inborn trait? Can it be discovered or enhanced through personal analysis or psychotherapy? To what extent is empathy teachable? All too often, the clinician is given the vague directive, "Go inward, young man!" and nothing more. Despite the emphasis on its centrality to the therapeutic process, the empathic process remains, for many, as mystifying as ever.

The demystification of the empathic process stands out as a primary goal in this volume. We submit that empathic ability—like intellectual, musical, or athletic ability—may well be in large measure a function of genetic inheritance in conjunction with life experience, especially early life experience. We strongly agree with the widespread consensus that personal analysis or psychotherapy is enormously valuable in potentiating innate empathic sensitivity. All these factors, however, do not preclude the importance of clinical training and instruction in the development of empathic ability. We shall delineate the various elements of the empathic process and hope thereby to increase the reader's opportunity for learning the inner workings of this mysterious phenomenon.

Our study of the empathic process has inexorably led us in the direction of countertransference theory and, along the way, to an equally intensive study of the phenomenon of projective identification. We use the term countertransference theory as one uses the term psychoanalytic theory, recognizing that it encompasses a spectrum of positions that are often contradictory. Our position on countertransference theory falls firmly within the totalist (Kernberg, 1965)—as opposed to the classical—perspective, the former approach holding that countertransference, broadly defined as the totality of the therapist's experience of the patient, represents a *potentially* useful tool in coming to understand the patient and in furthering the objectives of the treatment. Within the tradition exemplified by what Gill (1983) has referred to as the "interpersonal paradigm of psychoanalysis," we maintain that psychoanalytic therapy is a radically mutual process fully involving two individuals who exert a mutual and ongoing influence upon one another. Far from seeking to become a blank screen, impervious to the patient's influence, the well-functioning therapist strives to appreciate the ways in which he is being *acted upon* by the patient. Sandler's (1976) idea that a compromise exists between the therapist's unique personality makeup and the patient's ability to infuse the therapeutic relationship with his own particular wishes and needs is especially useful in assessing the degree of influence exerted by the therapeutic interaction upon the self-experience of the therapist.

Insufficient recognition of the way in which the therapist is acted upon by the patient has contributed to a failure to appreciate the relationship between empathy and projective identification. In the pages that follow, we propose to expand upon our earlier formulation (Tansey and Burke, 1985) that the mechanism of projective identification from the patient is always involved in the therapist's achieving empathic contact; and, conversely, that when a patient engages in projective identification, there is always the potential for the therapist to achieve an empathic outcome, whether or not this potential is actualized. Although empathy and projective identification have often been thought to be unrelated—if not downright antipathetic—we intend to develop our position further that they represent intimately related aspects of a unitary sequence for the therapist's processing of "interactional communications." By interactional communications, we mean all communications, both in words and in actions, that are transmitted consciously and unconsciously through the interaction by both patient and therapist. Because projective identification from a patient has the potential to lead to the stormy countertransference developments with which it is typically associated, we also shall broaden the scope of our previous examination (Burke and Tansey, 1985) of disruptions in the empathic process.

Numerous authors—notable among them Ogden (1979, 1982) and Gill (1984)—have emphasized the need for a redefinition of traditional psychoanalytic concepts in order to integrate interpersonal and intrapsychic perspectives. Empathy, projective identification, and countertransference are three major bridging concepts that include both intrapsychic and interpersonal elements. We shall elucidate the interrelationship between these concepts by specifying the reciprocal influences of the interpersonal field and the intrapsychic experience for each of the three phenomena.

The format of the book is as follows. Chapter 2 presents an historical review and synthesis of the psychoanalytic literature dealing with the concepts of empathy, projective identification, and countertransference, which have frequently been considered separate and unrelated aspects of the therapist's identificatory experience. In arriving at a different conclusion, we trace the historical progression of stages in the understanding of the therapist's identificatory experience. This progression began with the acknowledgment (which took nearly 40 years to accomplish) that a therapist often responds with powerful emotions to his work with given patients and that this reaction does not necessarily indicate a pathological impingement from the therapist on the therapeutic process. The literature continued to evolve through the late 1940s and 1950s in the direction of emphasizing the potential usefulness of such powerful emotional responses. More recently, major efforts have been made to specify the varieties of countertransference experience. Having reviewed some of the gross and subtle distinctions in the uses of various terms, chapter 3 provides careful definitions of important terms as we are using them so as to obviate confusion. In addition, we elaborate our position that complementary identifications on the therapist's part are to be included in the empathic process, and we discuss what we consider to be the intimate relationship between empathy and projective identification.

Chapters 4–7 present an expanded version of our unitary sequence for the processing of interactional communications. We propose a schema—rather than a cookbook recipe—that details the phases and subphases whereby a therapist receives a patient's projective identification, processes it internally, and then communicates, both verbally and nonverbally, to the patient. With many brief clinical vignettes, there is extensive discussion of the countertransference experience as it may lead both to productive empathic outcomes and to disruptions in the empathic process. Specific subphases afford a comprehensive understanding of where disruptions may occur and how they can be addressed.

Validation of clinical hypotheses—whether countertransference based or not—is an area of glaring weakness in the psychoanalytic literature. In chapter 8, this thorny and elusive matter is examined. The simple fact that a therapist experiences one affective state or another while working with a given patient is by no means a guarantee that this feeling is in any way a useful tool for understanding the patient better. The effort to make sense of clinical material—including but not limited to countertransference material—is inescapably an inferential, hermeneutical enterprise. We divide countertransference-based hypotheses into two categories—those which pertain to the determination of the source of the countertransference experience and those which pertain to the underlying meanings for the patient of the countertransference experience. Following upon Schafer's (1954) recommendations relative to the interpretation of Rorschach inkblot responses, we propose five "lines of inference" for each category of validation (source and meaning). Among the five lines of inference, the therapist must seek converging support for his hypotheses.

Chapter 9 focuses on the uses and abuses of countertransference disclosure to a patient. We review the psychoanalytic debate over countertransference disclosure as well as the accompanying technical and theoretical implications. In keeping with the consistent attempt throughout this volume to move back and forth between theoretical abstraction and the nuts-and-bolts of everyday clinical implementation, we differentiate useful from disruptive countertransference-based interventions by concentrating on the preparation, implementation, and ultimate impact of disclosive interventions.

Chapter 10 comprises three extended clinical vignettes that operationalize, in very concrete terms, the unfolding of the empathic process. All three are difficult cases, involving powerful projective identifications from patients contributing to countertransference responses which are problematic. In closing, chapter 11 pulls together the various threads of this volume and suggests some new directions for future efforts.

The consultant in our opening vignette was not the Delphic oracle, but rather a gifted clinician who had learned to absorb material in a variety of different ways and to direct his "evenly hovering attention" not only to information coming from the outside but also to subtle responses emanating from within. This book is written not only for young clinicians whose needs are obvious, but also for experienced clinicians who are interested in methodological guidelines for becoming more systematic in teaching, supervision, and the objective scrutiny of their own subjective experience.

2 Countertransference, Empathy, and Projective Identification

An Historical Perspective

Examinations of the experience of the psychoanalytic therapist have traditionally fallen under the heading of countertransference and—for those authors who make this distinction—noncountertransference. The clinical processes of empathy and of projective identification also figure prominently in efforts to understand the arousal of identificatory experiences for the therapist. Whereas empathy is typically related to a therapist's skillful functioning, projective identification is commonly associated with countertransference turmoil. In subsequent chapters we develop the argument that the processes of empathy and projective identification, far from being unrelated or even antipathetic, are in fact intimately related in a way that is critical to the fullest possible understanding of countertransference responses to virtually all patients. The strongest and most obvious link between empathy, projective identification, and countertransference is that all three involve the arousal of an identificatory experience—whether transient or enduring—on the part of the therapist.

Our intention here in the present chapter is to trace major historical trends in psychoanalytic approaches to countertransference theory. The historical development of this literature comprises three stages. First, clinicians and theoreticians, struggling with the goal of "scientific objectivity," had to acknowledge that identificatory experiences for the therapist—even those of a powerful nature—occur with regularity. This acknowledgment made possible subsequent efforts to use the emotional experiences of the therapist constructively within the treatment. The progression has culminated in current attempts to specify the varieties of countertransference experience with increasing clarity.

Advances in psychoanalytic understanding of the identificatory experience of the therapist-in-interaction have frequently come as the result of mutually enriching cross-fertilization between the theoretical developments of empathy, projective identification, and countertransference. This enrichment has occurred despite the frequent involvement of opposing theoretical perspectives within the psychoanalytic community. In his 1965 review of the countertransference literature, Kernberg distinguished between the "classical" and the "totalist" approaches to countertransference. The former restricts the concept of countertransference to the therapist's unconscious, pathological reactions to the patient that reflect unresolved conflicts that need to be overcome in order for the therapist to work well with the patient. In contrast, the totalist approach broadens the concept to include the therapist's total response to the patient—conscious and unconscious, "real" and neurotically "distorted." The totalist camp argues further that the usual distinction between the therapist's so-called realistic perceptions and his neurotic perceptions is fallacious, since perceptions virtually always involve elements of past and present reality. The classicist views countertransference as a pathological impediment to be overcome; the totalist views it as a potentially useful tool for understanding the patient. As will become clear, the disagreement is partly substantive and partly attributable to different definitions of terms.

1910: FREUD'S SEEMINGLY CONTRADICTORY VIEW OF COUNTERTRANSFERENCE

To understand the apparent schism that exists in countertransference theory, we must reexamine Freud's introduction of the term in 1910:

> We have become aware of the "counter-transference," which arises in the physician as a result of the patient's influence on his unconscious feelings, and we are almost inclined to insist that he shall recognize his counter-transference in himself and overcome it [p. 144].

The question arises as to what Freud meant by "overcoming" countertransference. Did he mean eliminate the countertransference response, which is to be regarded *only* as an impediment deriving solely from the analyst's unresolved conflicts; or did he mean attempt to analyze and understand the experience, thereby reducing its intensity? The first interpretation coincides with the classical view; the second accords with the totalist. In the same paper, Freud prescribed a self-analysis for the analyst, stating that "anyone who fails to produce results in a self-analysis of this kind may at once give up any idea of being able to treat patients by analysis" (p. 145).

Beyond these initial penetrating comments, Freud wrote very little on countertransference. In his 1912 technical paper, he alluded to the subject in the following widely quoted passage:

> I cannot advise my colleagues too urgently to model themselves during psychoanalytic treatment on the surgeon, who puts aside all his feelings, even his human sympathy, and concentrates his mental forces on the single aim of performing the operation as skillfully as possible . . . . The justification for requiring this emotional coldness is that it creates the most advantageous conditions for both parties: for the doctor a desirable protection for his own emotional life and for the patient the largest amount of help we can give him today [p. 115].

Both of the foregoing passages are invoked as support for the classical view. A case can be made, however, that Freud's writings also contain the seeds for the totalist perspective on countertransference, defined broadly as the therapist's total response to the patient.

For example, in the two paragraphs that immediately follow the suggestion that the analyst emulate the surgeon, Freud argued that in attempting to make sense of the patient's material, the analyst must not substitute a "censorship of his own for the selection that the patient has forgone." Instead, the analyst must strive to "turn his own unconscious like a receptive organ toward the transmitting unconscious of the patient." He then appeared to contradict rather sharply his recommendation that the therapist "put aside all his feelings":

> But if the doctor is to be in a position to use his unconscious in this way as an instrument in the analysis, he must fulfill one psychological condition to a high degree. He may not tolerate any resistances in himself which hold back from his consciousness what has been perceived by his unconscious; otherwise he would introduce into the analysis a new species of selection and distortion which would be far more detrimental than that resulting from concentration of attention [p. 116].

Thus it appears that in the space of a few sentences, Freud supported both sides of the debate. On the one hand, he recommended that the therapist model himself after the surgeon and sweep aside all emotional reactions in an effort to achieve "emotional coldness." But he also urged the therapist to attend to his perceptions as fully as he is able.

What is to be made of this apparent contradiction? Guntrip (1971), in discussing the observation that "Freud is the easiest writer to make contradict himself" (p. 5) saw such contradictions as a consequence of Freud's being a true "pioneer," the first to explore conflictual areas of the mind in a systematic fashion.

Returning to Freud's (1912) paper, however, we may find a resolution to this apparent contradiction. Immediately following the last passage, he "insisted" that the aspiring analyst himself undergo a "psychoanalytic purification" through a personal analysis so as to eliminate what Stekel (1911) had termed "blind spots." In so doing, Freud moved from the suggestion of self-analysis to that of actually seeking out an analyst for personal treatment. The contradiction may therefore be resolved on the basis of the Freud's assumption that an analyst could become purified of contaminating personal issues and thus become essentially a perfect conduit through which conscious and unconscious perceptions of the patient can then flow. Like the surgeon, he would then be able to put aside *his own* feelings without having to "hold back from consciousness what has been perceived by his unconscious," since those perceptions would reflect *only* the patient and contain no subjective distortion whatsoever.

Freud's belief, in the early days of psychoanalysis, that a permanent and thorough "psychoanalytic purification" was possible did not hold up under subsequent experience. In an explicit recognition of this fact some 25 years later, Freud (1937) himself suggested that the analyst return to the couch every five years for additional treatment. He compared the analyst's constant bombardment with his patient's primitive material to that of the X-ray technician, who must take "special precautions" to avoid untoward effects. For the analyst, among the "dangers of analysis" is the constant threat that contact with the patient might stir up "all the instinctual demands which he would otherwise keep under suppression" (p. 249). Thus, Freud concluded not only for patients but for analysts-as-patients themselves, the process of analysis is in fact both terminable (generally on grounds of practicality) and interminable (in terms of the need for ongoing self-examination).

Freud's early optimism for thorough and permanent psychoanalytic purification for prospective analysts evolved to a much more conservative—some would say pessimistic—position on the efficacy of psychoanalytic treatment. This transformation held important implications for countertransference theory. Although Freud reversed his position on transference from viewing it only as a danger to regarding it as a potentially indispensable tool, he never modified his thinking on countertransference in the same way. Even in his final words on the subject, his emphasis was on the analyst's seeking continuing treatment so as to be able to control his own suppressed instincts despite the X-ray-like bombardment of working with patients. Although the seeds of the totalist view of countertransference as potentially useful may be found in Freud, this idea never achieved full fruition in his work. The idea of countertransference as an impediment continued to hold sway over the notion that a therapist can make potentially good use of a strong emotional reaction to a patient.

1910–1948: FOUR DECADES OF SILENCE

Apart from the papers already mentioned, Freud went no further in the exploration of countertransference. Not until the late 1940s was the subject taken up in the literature with any depth or substance. Various opinions have been offered to account for the enormous hiatus of nearly 40 years from the introduction of the term until its active exploration in the literature.

Roland (1981) offered two factors to account for this gap. First, psychoanalysis wished to differentiate itself as fully as possible from "unscientific" artistic and literary efforts to probe the human mind, since these approaches tended to emphasize the occult. Second, the absence of countertransference studies reflected the desire for a strictly objective stance on the part of analysts so as not to submit patients to the harsh Victorian morality that prevailed at that time.

We might extend Roland's observation still further regarding the psychoanalytic reaction to Victorian judgmentalism. By not attending to countertransference, analysts may or may not have spared their patients from having to submit to moralistic expectations. But it appears that they did not direct a similarly accepting attitude toward themselves in the conduct of their own work. That is to say, the prevailing expectation of strict analytic objectivity, departures from which were viewed as essentially pathological and "bad," in and of itself seems unmistakably harsh and Victorian.

In a very important paper written in 1957, Racker attributed the 40-year neglect of countertransference to a persistence of infantile ideals passed along from one generation of analysts to the next. The training analysis represented the primary vehicle for this legacy, characterized by the analyst's colluding unconsciously with the analysand's infantile idealization of him. The training analyst's failure to handle countertransference more effectively resulted in the candidate's feeling enormous pressure to live up to similar standards of "perfection" with his own patients, thus perpetuating the "myth of the analytic situation" that analysis is "an interaction between a sick person and healthy one" (p. 308). Racker argued that transference had been much more carefully studied than countertransference for the same reason that the Oedipus complex of the child toward his parents had been much more closely examined than that of the parents toward their child.

If indeed Racker's argument is valid that the 40-year neglect of countertransference represented a psychoanalytic heritage passed from one generation to the next, it follows that this legacy was set in motion by Freud himself. This conclusion is perfectly consistent with Freud's relative neglect of the subject in his clinical papers. It is also consistent with Freud's training and experience in the hard sciences prior to his founding the psychoanalytic movement. Like a surgeon or a laboratory scientist, the "objective" analyst was expected to strive to establish a sterile field for the patient, uncontaminated by the therapist's personal material.

During those 40 years of virtual inactivity, Freud's early followers (Ferenczi, 1919; Simmel, 1926) maintained what we (Tansey and Burke, 1985) have previously referred to as the "poltergeist view" of countertransference as something dangerous that needs to be controlled. There are, however, two exceptions during this hiatus that point to the potential usefulness of the therapist's emotional response to the patient. Both of these contributions are remarkably prescient in anticipating the totalist viewpoint.

The first is an exceptionally illuminating paper by Deutsch (1926) in which she introduced but did not fully elaborate the notion that there are two types of identifications involved in the therapist's experience of the patient. Her regrettably brief comments on countertransference are embedded within a paper that attempts to utilize psychoanalytic insights to shed light on occult processes. In the very first such statement that we know of in the literature, Deutsch argued that countertransference includes not only pathological responses but also the process of unconcious identification with a patient through revival of memory traces from the analyst's own developmental experiences that are similar to those of the patient. It is this identificatory process that forms the basis of "intuitive empathy." Deutsch also pointed out that countertransference is not limited to the analyst's identification with the patient's ego—what Racker (1957) much later referred to as "concordant" identifications—but also entailed identification with the patient's "original objects." She called this the analyst's "complementary attitude" and believed that it arose from the patient's directing toward the analyst the same "infantile-libidinous wishes" that were once directed toward the patient's parents. For Deutsch, *both* types of identification form the basis of intuitive empathy.

Virtually everyone who has written on this subject disagrees with Deutsch's observation that complementary identifications are included in the empathic process. The consensus is to consider only the analyst's identification with the patient's self as characteristic of empathy, not the identifications with the patient's internalized objects. Nearly 60 years after Deutsch's paper, we (Tansey and Burke, 1985) independently arrived at the same conclusion that both forms of identification are to be considered as trial identifications that potentially may lead toward an empathic outcome. We did this without being aware that Deutsch had made the same point.

Deutsch went on to specify various forms of countertransference "short-circuiting" that arise from the analyst's failure to utilize and master his acquired identifications. One must wonder if her extraordinarily insightful comments were compressed into the space of three short pages because she realized that she was clashing head-on with the one-sided view of countertransference as strictly pathological that prevailed in 1926.

Whereas Deutsch's contribution was regrettably brief, Reik (1937) wrote an entire book on the subject of the therapist's use of his affective response to the patient. He took this same book, entitled *Surprise and the Psychoanalyst,* essentially in its entirety, modified some of the chapters, and added more than 20 new chapters in his 1948 *Listening with the Third Ear.* He did not use the term countertransference in either book, and it is perhaps largely for this reason that he is not mentioned in any of the major reviews of the countertransference literature (Kernberg, 1965; Langs, 1976; Epstein and Feiner, 1979). Nevertheless, we argue that his work holds very special significance for countertransference theory since he ardently encouraged the therapist to attend to affective signals emanating from within as vital sources of information for comprehending the patient's unconscious processes. Although Fliess (1942) generally receives credit for describing the process of "trial identification" that underlies the empathic process, Reik (1937) presented a similar description five years earlier.

> The united or conflicting effect of the [patient's] words, gestures, and unconscious signals, which point to the existence of certain hidden impulses and ideas, will certainly not at first stimulate the observing analyst to psychological comprehension. Their first effect will rather be to rouse in himself unconsciously impulses and ideas with a like tendency. The unconscious reception of the signals will *not at first result in their interpretation, but in the induction [in the analyst] of the hidden impulses and emotions that underlie them,* [p. 193].
>
> The other person's impulse, which has unconsciously aroused a corresponding impulse in the observer, is seen externally like the image on the retina. The observation of other people's suppressed and repressed impulses is only possible by the roundabout way of inner perception. In order to comprehend the unconscious of another person, we must, at least for a moment, change ourselves into and become that person [p. 199].

Reik argued against calling this transformation within the analyst an identification; he suggested instead that it be considered a "temporary introjection" (p. 199). The communicative process that Reik described goes on unconsciously both for the patient and for the analyst. It is only by attending to the affective signals coming from within himself that the analyst is able to fathom their hidden meanings and to bring into his own consciousness what the patient is unconsciously communicating about himself through this inductive process. Reik went into extensive detail, augmented by rich clinical illustrations, describing how the analyst achieves insight both about the patient and about himself by paying attention to his own subtle affective responses to the patient.

In commenting on his work, Annie Reich (1960) maintained that Reik was not describing the utilization of countertransference, which she defined in its narrow and pathological sense, since the transient introjection of the patient remained controlled and temporary. She stated that Reik was referring to processes in which "the analyst never loses sight of the patient as a separate being and at no time feels his own identity changed [which] enables him to remain uninvolved" (p. 391). Although her position is defensible in reference to Reik's (1937) earlier contribution, her claim that Reik was referring to rather mild emotional reactions on the analyst's part does not appear to be accurate in reference to his later volume, to which we shall return later.

Building on the work of Reik, Fliess (1942) studied the manner in which the analyst uses his self-experiences with patients to act as the "telephone receiver" (Freud, 1912) of the patient's unconscious. Comparing the analyst to a "tea taster," Fliess believed that the optimally functioning analyst temporarily introjected the "instinctual material" emanating from the patient, experiencing its quality but not its intensity. Referring to the experience of temporarily "becoming the subject himself" as transient "trial identification," Fliess explicitly disagreed with Reik's position that such experiences should properly be labeled temporary introjections and not identifications. Despite terminological differences, Fliess's position appears to be entirely harmonious with Reik's from a conceptual point of view. Fliess believed that through analysis of the empathic trial identification, the analyst could obtain "inside knowledge" of the patient that was unavailable by other means. He described a sequence of events in which the therapist's "work ego" allowed him to receive the patient's communications, engage in trial identifications, and observe and analyze the entire process, all the while remaining in control and retaining a firm sense of separateness from the patient.

In Fliess's conceptualization of empathy, the feelings experienced by the therapist during the trial identification were the patient's feelings. The therapist merely utilized his capacity transiently to "become the subject." This experience was viewed as distinctly different from countertransference, which Fliess described as an uncontrolled surrender to the "induced striving" on the therapist's part. For Fliess, countertransference produced a more permanent condition, rendering the analyst ineffective as the neutral observer of the analytic process.

In a subsequent paper, Fliess (1953) widened the dichotomy between empathy and countertransference still further. Whereas the empathic experience was characterized by the analyst's taking in identifications from the patient, countertransference by contrast involved a reawakening in the therapist of identifications from his own traumatic past having nothing at all to do with the patient. As such, countertransference for

Fliess was a "danger situation" (Freud, 1937) that contaminated the "sterile field" of the therapeutic interaction. Fliess left unexplored how one determined the extent to which the experiential state of the therapist accurately or truly reflected the patient's internal world.

Fliess's elucidation of the empathic process seemed to have struck a compromise that was acceptable to mainstream psychoanalysis in resolving the dilemma confronting the analyst, who was expected to be both detached from and yet emotionally sensitive to his patient's unconscious communications. Within the context of drive theory, this compromise was possible because of his strong emphasis on the therapist's trial identification with his patient as a brief contact with the patient's "instinctualized material," which remained low in intensity and was rapidly neutralized. The therapist always remained in full control of the impulses aroused. In conjunction with Reik's earlier work, Fliess's emphasis on the usefulness of emotional responses to a patient—albeit responses that are highly circumscribed in time and in intensity—appears to have helped lay the groundwork for the extreme upsurge of interest in countertransference that occurred around 1950.

In addition, three other influences established a foundation for the imminent upsurge of interest in countertransference: the development of object relations theory in England, the burgeoning interpersonal psychoanalysis movement in America, and the widening application of psychoanalytic theory and practice to the treatment of children and severely disturbed adults.

The object relations theorists during the 1930s and 1940s provided a major shift in developmental theory from a "drive/structure" model to a "relational/structure" model (Greenberg and Mitchell, 1983). A reconceptualization of developmental theory from the object relations perspective expanded the view of human development by considering the influence of interpersonal experience. Especially in the work of Winnicott (1936, 1945), the external, real-life objects with whom the growing infant and child interacted were seen as contributing significantly to the gradual differentiation and integration of internal self- and object representations in the child's psychic makeup.

Other major object relations theorists of this time period, such as Fairbairn (1946) and Balint (1937), were making important contributions. But the work of Melanie Klein (1946, 1955) undoubtedly exerted the greatest impact. Unlike Winnicott, however, Klein remained firmly intrapsychic in her focus. Focusing on the child's efforts to adapt to and defend against instinctual drives emanating from within, she virtually ignored the impact of real, external objects on the child's developmental experience. In Klein's language, an object referred not to an actual, external, real-life figure, but rather to an internalized mental representation of that object. Any resemblance, or lack of it, between the two was of no consequence or interest to Klein. With regard to the clinical setting also, she maintained the same intrapsychic focus on the patient, not attending to countertransference except to comment in passing on its hindrance to treatment.

In 1946, Klein introduced the concept of projective identification as a defense mechanism by which the infant attempts to rid the self of destructive, aggressive impulses by projecting these impulses in fantasy into an internalized object, which in turn is experienced as persecutory. By controlling the object, the infant then feels a sense of control over its own instinctual aggression. The threat is felt to be coming from the outside rather than from the inside. The concept the projective identification has since been used in a variety of different and often confusing ways. As Sandler (1987) has emphasized in an extremely useful and lucid account, Klein was referring to a process that occurs *in fantasy only*. In Klein's definition of projective identification, external objects are *not* regarded as actually being affected interpersonally. Only internal or fantasy objects are influenced. Sandler refers to this usage as "first stage projective identification."

It remained the task of subsequent object relations theorists to extend the work of Klein both to an exploration of the in fluence of actual interactions with real objects on the child's psychological development and to an examination of the therapist's countertransference as influenced by the patient's projective identification. As Sandler points out, Heimann (1950), Racker (1968), and Grinberg (1962) used the concept of projective identification to refer to the patient's *actual influence* in causing the therapist to identify with either the patient's internalized self or object representations. Thus, the strictly fantasy activity involved in Klein's usage of projective identification becomes actualized to some degree in the form of real influence over the therapist's countertransference status—what Sandler refers to as "second stage projective identification."

Despite the fact that Klein herself remained staunchly intrapsychic in her theory building, her work contained the seeds of several new and critical advances in clinical theory and practice and helped to set the stage for the totalist viewpoint. The extension of her work by her followers provided a theoretical underpinning from which to extend the concept of empathy, which had been thought to be characterized only by brief and mild emotional responses, to include much more powerful and often negative responses. As Ogden (1979) pointed out, the development of the concept of projective identification by Klein's followers shifted from the intrapsychic to the interpersonal arena and, as such, provided a very useful bridge between the two realms. The concept of projective identification also provided the theoretical groundwork for the therapist to make use of strong, and often negative, reactions to a patient. Prior to the development of object relations theory, strong emotional responses were generally regarded not as empathic reflections of the patient's emotions but as impure impediments indicating pathological countertransference. The majority of the early totalist theorists, including Winnicott (1965), Little (1951), Heimann (1950), and Racker (1957), were heavily influenced by Klein.

Although geographically separate, the interpersonal psychoanalysis movement in America during the 1930s and 1940s shared some common ground with the object relations school. Led by Sullivan (1930, 1931, 1936, 1938, 1940, 1953) and Fromm (1941, 1947, 1955), the emphasis shifted from intrapsychic drives and defenses to the interpersonal and sociocultural realms. Sullivan's pioneering work on the "interpersonal field theory" combined a respect for intrapsychic forces with a bold new interpretation of psychopathology as a humanly understable adaptation to a less than optimal environment. Espousing a philosophy that attempted to take the onus away from "mental illness" and preferring instead to speak of universal "difficulties in living," he argued that we are all much more simply human than otherwise. Sullivan, unlike Klein, placed central importance on the quality of past interpersonal relationships in the formation of personality and the manner in which interpersonal anxiety is dealt with. Fromm's view of the impact of societal and cultural forces on individual choice provided an even wider scope of influence on personality development than Sullivan's.

Interpersonal psychoanalysis diverged from drive theory in two important ways. First, variables other than intrapsychic drives were viewed as important and active determinants of personality development and functioning that required acknowledgment and investigation. Second, rather than considering psychotherapy as occurring in a sterile field uncontaminated by the perspective of the therapist, the interpersonalists viewed treatment as a two-person interaction in which the therapist is both participant and observer. As a "participant-observer," the therapist influenced and formed part of what was observed. Treatment was no longer considered to be the therapist's detached, uninvolved observation of the pathological intrapsychic operations of the patient. The therapist's experience of the patient was valued as an important source of information about the patient and the therapeutic relationship.

In addition to advancements in the theory of empathy, the development of object relations theory, and the growth of interpersonal psychoanalysis, a fourth factor helped to set the stage for the reawakening of countertransference theory beginning in 1948. We are referring to the widening application of psychoanalytic theory and practice to include both children and more disturbed adult clinical populations. Melanie Klein and Anna Freud were the dominant leaders in psychoanalytic work with children, and Sullivan (1931) pioneered in the treatment of psychotic and schizophrenic patients. It was discovered that the psychotherapy of both groups usually exerts a greater emotional impact on the therapist than work with neurotic adult patients. Channels of communication are more often nonverbal and action oriented, with a greater emotional pressure being placed on the therapist for responsivity and affective participation. As a consequence, the emotional reactions of the therapist working with the child or the severely disturbed adult demand greater attention. Such responses, if properly handled can be extremely useful sources of understanding the patient.

1948–1958: THE ERUPTION OF INTEREST IN COUNTERTRANSFERENCE

The period 1948–1958 represents a critical breakthrough for countertransference theory and, as a consequence, for psychoanalytic theory in general. Having incubated in a half-century of clinical work with patients, the idea burst forth in full force from several quarters that the analyst could potentially make very good use of strong emotional reactions to a patient.

Heimann (1950) is widely cited as having made the landmark statement of the totalist perspective. She described the analytic situation as "a *relationship* between two persons" (p. 81) characterized by the presence of strong feelings in both partners. She argued that the term countertransference should properly refer to all the feelings that the therapist has for the patient, since the distinction between "realistic" responses and "distorted" responses based on past experiences is a very difficult one to make. She applied the same argument to the term transference. Believing that Freud himself had been misread on countertransference strictly as a source of disturbance, Heimann asserted that the key to utilizing strong emotional reactions was for the analyst to "*sustain* the feelings which are stirred in him, as opposed to discharging them (as the patient does), in order to *subordinate* them to the analytic task" (p. 81). She posited that the "analyst's unconscious understands that of his patient" on a much deeper and more accurate level than the analyst's conscious reasoning. By attending to "feelings roused in himself with his patient's associations and behavior," the analyst is best able to be reached by the "patient's voice" (p. 82).

Although Heimann's brief paper is noteworthy for its clarity and usefulness, Reik (1948) had covered much the same territory two years before Heimann's paper. Nonetheless, throughout the countertransference literature, Reik's work is consistently overlooked. In addition to the fact that he himself did not use the actual term countertransference, the general neglect of his work may be attributable to his having been a psychologist who immigrated from Germany to America, where psychoanalysis was still dominated by the medical profession.

In comparison to his earlier efforts, Reik's work in 1948 became considerably bolder. Borrowing from Neitzsche, he stated that an analyst must learn to "listen with the third ear" in order to understand the unconscious of his patient. With language very similar to Heimann's (1950) but in much more elaborate detail, Reik urged analysts to attend very carefully to "inner voices" that signal the analyst's unconscious perceptions about the patient. Impressions that typically might be regarded as insignificant became, for Reik, far more important than the logical, "objective" reasoning processes that had come to dominate the approach of many analysts. Like Heimann, he believed that affective reactions to a patient, whether subtle or gross, were the manifestations of the analyst's unconscious perception, which potentially is far more attuned to the patient than his conscious perception. It is this unconscious perception that must lead the way.

Just as Heimann (1950) emphasized that the analyst must not become "a mechanical brain which can produce interpretations on the basis of a purely intellectual procedure" (p. 81), Reik referred to the analytic "worship of the bitch-goddess objectivity, of pseudo precision, of facts and figures," (p. 147) and of analysts' fears of writing of their own reactions to patients. He believed that "objectivity" had become confused with inhumanness, and he, too, pointed out that emotions could be aroused without being expressed or acted upon. Though he did not label strong responses as countertransference, Reik (1948) wrote:

> What kind of psychoanalyst, some readers will ask, can feel annoyed or impatient? Is this the much-praised calm and the correct scientific attitude of the therapist? Is this the pure mirror that reflects the image of the patient who comes to psychoanalysis with his troubles, symptoms, and complaints? Is this the proper couch-side manner? The question is easily answered. The psychoanalyst is a human being like any other and not a god. There is nothing superhuman about him. In fact, he has to be human. How else could he understand other human beings? . . . If he were cold and unfeeling, a "stuffed shirt" as some

> plays portray him, he would be an analytic robot or a pompous, dignified ass who could not gain entry to the secrets of the human soul [p. 154].

According to Reik, human sensitivity in no way contradicts therapeutic objectivity; in a well-functioning analyst, the two peacefully coexist.

Several other papers appeared almost simultaneously that are important to mention. Winnicott (1949) published a paper whose very title, "Hate in the Countertransference," conveyed a radical position for that time. The paper referred to analytic work with severely disturbed patients and emphasized the need for a treatment to provide protection from abuse, not only for the patient but also for the therapist. Such measures would provide necessary relief for the therapist and reduce the pressure to act on strong and often negative emotional feelings and urges aroused by the patient.

Berman (1949) is cited in an opening footnote to Heimann's paper because of his similar position, though neither had been aware of the other's work at the time of writing. Berman's paper is also noteworthy in that, unlike Heimann, he favored the judicious usage of countertransference disclosure, a technical recommendation that was further supported by Little (1951). Although Little retained the narrow, classical definition of countertransference as a response based on past experience, she managed to do so with a remarkably tolerant view of the analyst as a human being. She believed that countertransference developments were inevitable but could be put to good use. She argued against a "paranoid or phobic attitude" toward countertransference and favored a "lessening of the didactic or authoritarian attitude" in the analyst. Tower (1956) pursued a similar line of thought, suggesting that analysts were more highly resistant to the awareness of countertransference than patients were of transference. In part, she attributed this to the "rigidity and prohibitiveness" of training institutes.

No single author has made more valuable contributions to the countertransference literature than Racker (1953, 1957). In rich clinical detail, he illustrated the manner in which a therapist could be induced by his patient to identify either with the patient's self, which he termed a concordant identification, or with the patient's internalized objects, which, following Deutsch (1926), he termed a complementary identification. He argued that although concordant identifications alone constituted the basis of empathy, both forms of identification should be considered countertransference in its totalistic sense. Referring to the talionic law, he asserted that every transference situation provokes a corresponding countertransference response. Analogous to the manner in which Freud depicted transference as both the greatest danger and the best tool for analytic work, Racker argued that the induced countertransference response, in addition to being a potentially serious barrier, could also be extremely valuable to the analyst, opening up avenues to understanding the patient that otherwise would simply not exist.

The key, according to Racker, is for the analyst to strive to maintain a "deep and continuous" contact with himself so as to be as aware as possible of his countertransference position in relation to the patient. Through this awareness, the analyst is better able to avoid falling into a blind repetition of the particular vicious circle that constitutes the patient's primary problem in human relationships. The awareness of countertransference lays the groundwork for the interpretation of the patient's unconscious efforts to repeat, leading to an interruption of the vicious circle and an opportunity to internalize a more positive outcome with the therapist. This in turn allows for more productive experiences in outside relationships and less pressure to repeat traumatic relationships. Without countertransference awareness, Racker insisted, the analyst was likely doomed to "drown" in his responses to the patient and destructively repeat the patient's vicious circle. He gave examples of therapists who had begun to succumb to forceful countertransference pressures and yet were eventually able to right themselves through self-awareness, ultimately snatching therapeutic victory from the jaws of defeat.

In opposition to the proliferation of publications espousing the potential usefulness of countertransference, papers began to appear from the so-called classical camp reemphasizing the view that strong emotional reactions by the analyst were to be viewed strictly as a problem. Fliess (1953) was representative of this group. He provided clinical examples in which he concluded that various thoughts and feelings of a therapist had absolutely nothing to do with the patient or the interaction but rather were derived exclusively from the analyst's intrapsychic conflicts. As such, the material represented pathological interference that the analyst must strive to "abolish."

Annie Reich (1951, 1960, 1966) is generally regarded as having been the leading proponent of the classical view of countertransference during the early 50s. Building upon the works of Reik, Deutsch, and Fliess, Reich argued that a therapist may indeed learn something about what is going on in the patient's unconscious through an awareness of what is happening in the therapist's own mind through the process of empathic identification. She repeatedly emphasized in all of her papers, however, that the identification must be "partial and short-lived." If, on the contrary, the analyst begins to experience strong emotions, she believed this was evidence of countertransference, which she narrowly defined as the analyst's unresolved conflicts and concerns that have nothing at all to do with the patient. Emotional intensity, for Reich, became a critical distinguishing factor between useful empathic trial identifications and pathological countertransference. She (1960) specifically attacked Heimann's (1950) seminal contribution on the grounds that Heimann had not recognized that her perception of the patient in her clinical example had been obscured by what Reich believed were her own feelings, which had nothing to do with the patient. Although the validity of Heimann's perception of her patient is debatable, Reich nevertheless made the very useful argument that a therapist's hypotheses concerning a patient, based on emotional responses to the patient, require clinical validation. Without such a validating process, there is no way of knowing with any certainty whether, and to what degree, such hypotheses are correct or not.

Despite the fact that she is described as the leading proponent of the classical view, Reich herself appeared to waver on the position that strong emotional responses to a patient are *always* pathological. Indeed, in the conclusion of her first paper on the subject (1951) she equivocated rather confusingly by stating, "Countertransference is a necessary prerequisite of analysis. If it does not exist, the necessary talent and interest is lacking" (p. 31). Similarly, in the 1960 paper, she maintained,

"The countertransference as such is not helpful, but the readiness to acknowledge its existence and the ability to overcome it is" (p. 392). Freud too (1910) had used the same verb, "overcome." Once again, it is not clear what was meant by this term. One way in which a strong emotional response may be "overcome" is for the therapist to recognize it as being in some way meaningful. Through understanding the source of the feeling, the feeling itself often becomes much less intense and the temptation to discharge the feeling in action is also reduced. This particular interpretation of overcome tends to lessen the apparent substantive differences between both Reich and Freud in relation to the totalist perspective.

A review of the countertransference literature of this era reveals additional examples of what appear to be terminological rather than substantive differences between the classical and the totalist perspectives. On the totalist side, for example, Racker (1957) explicitly referred to the potential danger of "drowning" in countertransference, Heimann (1950) warned of the dangers of intense emotional responses, and a similar caveat was offered by Little (1951). On the classical side, Reich (1951) herself acknowledged that emotional responses to a patient may be very useful in illuminating the patient's unconscious.

Such instances of agreement do not diminish the differences between the two perspectives, especially regarding the intensity factor. Beyond a certain point, albeit vaguely defined, the classicist argues that an intense response to a patient has passed from the realm of useful trial identification into the realm of pathological countertransference emanating strictly from the analyst's own past history and having nothing to do with the patient. The totalist holds open not the certainty but the possibility that if the therapist is able to pull back and begin to examine the experience of even a strong response, there is the potential to learn something useful about the patient. Whereas the classicist may be too quick to attribute an intense response to the therapist's exclusively private concerns, the totalist runs the risk of too readily concluding that the countertransference response to the patient constitutes a royal road to the patient's unconscious rather than a detour into his own.

How is a therapist to know whether an emotional response to a patient, mild or intense, is a private problem or a useful clue? Clearly the matter rests with a process of clinical validation, an area in which too little has been written. We address this matter in considerable detail in chapter 8.

THE 1960s: THE SECOND HIATUS IN COUNTERTRANSFERENCE THEORY

Following the eruption of papers between 1948 and 1958, the literature on countertransference once again entered an extended period of dormancy. Although literature reviews appeared, there were no major milestones in the countertransference literature until the mid-1970s. Throughout this second hiatus in the development of countertransference theory, several important papers surfaced on the subjects of empathy and projective identification that examined the therapist's experience of the therapeutic interaction. We believe that the further refinements in the concepts of empathy and projective identification provided the groundwork for the second reawakening of interest in countertransference beginning in the mid-1970s.

Schafer (1959), Kohut (1959), and Greenson (1960) published seminal papers on the subject of empathy that continue to be cited today as major contributions to the literature. Kohut emphasized the important role of empathy as the therapist's mode of observation for scientific inquiry in psychoanalysis. From an ego psychological point of view, Schafer and Greenson examined the process through which a therapist undergoes an empathic identification that is reflective of the patient's experience. Schafer defined several aspects of the therapist's ego functioning required for the "controlled regression" that characterizes "generative empathy" and the concomitant "conflict free interplay of projective and introjective mechanisms" (p. 346). Whereas Schafer sketched a brief outline of the "mechanisms of generative empathy," Greenson built upon Fliess's (1942) initial efforts and went much further in delineating the sequence of events involved in the empathic process. In his concept of the internalized "working model" that the therapist develops of the patient over time and then utilizes to potentiate the empathic identification, Greenson provided a brilliant insight into the experiential nature of the therapist's introjective identification with his patient. Both Schafer and Greenson studied the empathic process from a primarily intrapsychic perspective centered on the structural capacities of the therapist's ego to engage in and manage affective identifications with a patient.

Following the papers by Kohut (1959), Schafer (1959), and Greenson (1960), the empathy literature became virtually inactive for the next decade. At the same time, work on projective identification became more active at this very time. Building upon papers by Bion (1955) and Racker (1957), Grinberg (1962) proposed the term "projective counteridentification" in direct response to the pressure of the patient's projective identification. Although he included projective identification as an "aspect" of countertransference, he very carefully distinguished projective counteridentification from "countertransference reactions resulting from the analyst's own emotional attitudes, or from his neurotic remnants, reactivated by the patient's conflicts" (p. 436).

Grinberg's contribution lay not only in coining a term to define this special aspect of countertransference, but also in his strong advocacy of projective counteridentification as potentially leading toward a greater (empathic) understanding of the patient: "Projective counter-identification may become a positive element in the analysis, since it clarifies to the analyst some of the patient's contents and attitudes, and makes possible certain interpretations, whose emergence could not otherwise be explained" (p. 440).

Malin and Grotstein (1966) were the first Americans to make a significant contribution to the understanding of projective identification. They attempted to delineate the manner in which the therapist's reception of the patient's projective identification formed "the basis of the therapeutic effect in psychoanalysis" (p. 26). In an examination of the relationship between projection and identification, they took the position that "all identification includes projection, and all projection includes identification" (p. 27). In the first such statement of its kind that we know of, they proposed that projective identification is "a normal, as well as abnormal, way of relating which persists into mature adulthood," the investigation of which can "enhance our knowledge of identification itself" (p. 27).

Taken together, the papers by Grinberg (1962) and by Malin and Grotstein (1966) advanced the overall exploration of the identification process occurring within the therapist in two important ways. First, because the authors viewed the identification process from the perspective of projective identification, they were able to emphasize the manner in which an identification is interpersonally induced. Rather than conceptualizing identification as a relatively static phenomenon involving exclusively intrapsychic events unfolding within the therapist, identification was definod as the outcome of an *interactional process* involving two participants. Second, contrary to the predominant view in the empathy literature, the analyst's potentially empathic identification with his patient was no longer portrayed as a comfortable, well-controlled experience. The authors took the position that the identificatory experience was often a very uncomfortable, poorly controlled response to the inductive pressure created by the patient's projective identification. Such experiences were no longer reflexively ascribed to pathological countertransference.

From 1968 to 1974, the empathy literature once again came to life with several significant contributions. Kohut's (1968, 1971) landmark work on the treatment of narcissistic character disorders placed the therapist's empathic ability into a central role in the therapeutic process. While most of his efforts focused on the influence of the therapist's empathic attitude on the developing idealized or mirror transference, Kohut (1971) cautioned therapists that the experience of being a selfobject is a difficult one indeed:

> In order to function properly during the analysis of such personality disorders the analyst must be capable of remaining interested in and attentive to the remobilized psychological structures despite the absence of significant object-instinctual cathexes. Furthermore, he must be capable of accepting the fact that his position (which is in harmony with the specific level of the major fixation) within the patient's therapeutically activated narcissistic world view is that of an archaic prestructural object, i.e., specifically, that of a function in the service of the maintenance of the patient's narcissistic equilibrium [p. 293–294].

Kohut's (1971, 1977) theory of psychic development and innovative technical recommendations served as a springboard for the increased interest in the perspective of self psychology and the role of empathy. Later authors (Wolf 1980; Goldberg, 1988) have continued to expand and deepen an understanding of the technical and theoretical aspects of the therapist's maintenance of an empathic attitude during the interaction with the patient, for whom the therapist is "an impersonal function related to the Kingdom of [the patient's] own remobilized narcissistic grandeur and exhibitionism" (Kohut, 1971 p. 288).

Olinick (1969) attempted to integrate the interactional focus of projective identification with the intrapsychic ego analysis characteristic of the empathy literature. He emphasized the therapeutic importance of the containment function that the therapist must serve for the patient's projections; thus the therapist must have a high level of "openness and receptivity." Borrowing from Kris (1952), he described the "ego operations" necessary for the therapist to engage in a therapeutic "regression in the service of the other" (p. 42).

In a follow-up paper, Olinick (1973) further specified the sequential functions of the therapist's "work ego" (Fliess, 1942). These functions are the basis for interpretation and for the "regressive experiencing of the regressed other as oneself, and oneself as the other" (p. 148). Olinick suggested that the therapist's reactions to the patient form a continuum (trial identification, counteridentification, overidentification) according to the degree of ego mastery of the experience. His efforts at differentiating a spectrum of possible countertransference responses presaged what we refer to as the "specifist" movement within the countertransference literature during the mid-1970s and the 1980s.

In a very enlightening paper, Beres and Arlow (1974) examined the relationship between empathy and intuition and discussed the role of fantasy activity in the empathic process. Pointing to identification followed by separation as being crucial to the empathic process, they explored the role of signal affect as the therapist's cue to shift from thinking and feeling *with* the patient to thinking *about* the patient. Although they did not use the term complementary identification, this is one of the very few papers that accords with Deutsch's (1926) position that such identifications, if properly handled, may indeed lead to an empathic outcome:

> The affect which the therapist experiences may correspond precisely to the mood which the patient has sought to stimulate in him as, for example, the masochist who tries to evoke criticism and attack. Empathy in such instances consists of recognizing that this is precisely what the patient wishes to provoke in the analyst. The affect experienced is a signal affect alerting the therapist to the patient's motivation and fantasy [p. 35].

In an examination of the dimensions of egocentricism and object centeredness in the identificatory experience of the therapist, Shapiro (1974) specified the "structural and adaptive mechanisms operative in the experience of empathy" (p. 7). Like Olinick's work, the paper anticipated the many papers that were forthcoming in the 1970s and 1980s in the countertransference literature seeking to distinguish between different categories of identification within the therapist.

THE 1970s AND 1980s: THE SPECIFIST MOVEMENT IN COUNTERTRANSFERENCE THEORY

Beginning in the 1970s, there has been a second reawakening of strong interest in countertransference that appears to have been stimulated by prior developments in the areas of empathy and projective identification. Although the number of publications on countertransference has increased since about 1974, a review of the literature reveals relatively fewer works dealing primarily with empathy or projective identification, with some notable exceptions (e.g., Buie, 1981; Ogden, 1979, 1982; Grotstein, 1981; Basch, 1983; Schafer, 1983; Sandler, 1987). The overall trend appears to be in the direction of classifying the therapist's identificatory experience as countertransference. Empathy and projective identification increasingly are being conceptualized as aspects of countertransference. In addition, as Epstein and Feiner (1979) have pointed out, fewer and fewer therapists believe that strong emotional reactions to a patient are *necessarily* pathological, a point of view that reflects an increasingly totalistic view of countertransference. Greenson (1974) is an outstanding example of a prominent classical analyst who shifted unequivocally to the totalist view of countertransference as potentially useful. Sandler (1976, 1987) and Gill (1983) are also noteworthy in this regard.

The totalist versus classical debate, so hotly waged during the 50s, has clearly subsided in favor of accepting and examining all of the experiences of the therapist as potentially—though not necessarily—useful. A recent and eloquent statement of this position is provided by Gorkin (1987). Questions about whether a therapist should or should not have a given reaction to his patient are less frequently raised. Rather, questions have been aimed at the specific kinds of identifications the therapist has undergone, the manner in which they arose in the therapeutic interaction, and their *degree of applicability* to the patient's concerns. The predominant view is that the therapist's identificatory experiences fall along a continuum ranging from identification directly reflective of the patient's concerns to those reflective of the therapist's idiosyncratic inclinations. Countertransference has become an all-inclusive term that is more and more frequently applied to the entire continuum.

The ambiguity and confusion that resulted from applying the term countertransference to such a broad range of experiences gave rise to a new breed of investigators whom we refer to as the "specifists." Their aim is to categorize and classify the varieties of identificatory experience for the therapist under the overarching rubric of countertransference. Although their numbers have proliferated in the past 10 to 15 years, Deutsch (1926), as mentioned earlier, appears to have made the first such distinction; she referred to empathic identifications with the patient's ego as opposed to empathic identifications with the patient's objects, which she termed complementary. Other early specifist efforts include Winnicott's (1949) objective versus idiosyncratic countertransference, Reich's (1951) sublimated versus pathological countertransference, and Racker's (1957) direct versus indirect countertransference. Cohen (1952) differentiated three types of countertransference responses arising from situational factors in the analyst's life, from the analyst's neurotic vulnerabilities, and from anxiety generated by the patient that the analyst has "incorporated in some manner." Benedek (1953) distinguished those countertransference responses arising in reaction to the transference of the patient from those stemming from the "analyst's projection of an important person of his past onto the patient"

(p. 206). The papers by Olinick (1973) and Shapiro (1974) previously alluded to should also be mentioned in the specifist tradition.

Since the early 1970s, the countertransference specifists have employed what appear to be five dimensions for differentiating types of therapist identifications: the degree of the therapist's consciousness or lack of consciousness of the experience; the degree of the therapist's control over the intensity of the experience; the degree of separateness or differentiation of ego boundaries maintained by the therapist through the different stages of the identificatory process; the type of introjection involved; and the question of whether the identification is with the patient's internalized self-representation (concordant identification) or with the patient's internalized object representation (complementary identification).

These dimensions provide the criteria for attempting to establish, along a continuum, the extent to which the therapist's identificatory experience is a reflection of the patient's internal world and a response to the interactional pressures exerted by the patient. At the opposite end of the continuum are those therapist identifications which may have been stimulated in the presence of the patient but emanate predominantly from the therapist's essentially private concerns. At best, the specifist tradition combines what is most useful from both the totalist and the classical perspectives. The former holds an openness to, and interest in, the potential usefulness of even strong emotional responses; the latter cautions against potential pitfalls and makes an effort to validate hypotheses.

Langs (1976) differentiated five "countertransference constellations" (p. 289), all of which were clearly demarcated from "primarily noncountertransference reactions." To distinguish sympathizing from empathizing, Liberman (1978) delineated six patient styles of communication, each of which elicit particular types of affective responses from the therapist that can be used to understand the patient's unconscious emotions. Chediak (1979) proposed that countertransference represents only one of five possible categories of therapist reactions, which also include intellectual understanding, a general response to the patient, the therapist's transference to the patient, and empathic identification. In his theory of "the intrapsychic nature of empathy," Buie (1981) proposed four types of perceptual referents that allow a therapist to complete the "inferential process" of knowing another person's subjective state: conceptualization, self-experience, resonance, and imaginative intuition.

In a useful specifist paper, Roland (1981) systematically categorized therapist identifications according to the degree of influence exerted by the patient. His five categories of "induced emotional reactions" included: transitory identifications with patients; preconscious associations and imagery; responses to a variety of transference experiences and situations created by the patient; responses that are part and parcel of a transference paradigm; and "countertransference proper," representing the analyst's unconscious problematic reactions usually to specific patients and transference situations.

Meissner (1982) formulated a model of transference-countertransference interaction based on a conceptualization of three developmental introjective configurations (aggressive, narcissistic, and erotic) of the borderline patient. He described the manner in which these configurations are reenacted within the therapeutic interaction, and he specified "reciprocal patterns of introjection and counterprojection in the analyst, which serve as the basis of countertransference reactions" (p. 121).

Finally, Lakovics (1983) discussed countertransference in an effort to provide useful guidelines for supervisors. He listed six sources of "total countertransference": concordant identifications, complementary identifications, interactional reactions, the therapist's life events, institutional countertransference, and classical countertransference.

SUMMARY

As we have attempted to demonstrate in this chapter, there have been a number of key historical developments in the psychoanalytic literature investigating countertransference, empathy, and projective identification as identificatory experiences within the therapist in the therapeutic interaction. The obvious first critical step had to involve acknowledgment that a therapist does indeed experience strong emotional responses with patients without this necessarily indicating emotional problems for the therapist. Given the early emphasis on surgical skill and scientific objectivity, this first step was very long in coming. The recognition of milder and usually positive feelings for a patient, officially sanctioned within mainstream psychoanalysis under the heading of "empathy," represented an important preliminary achievement leading to the acknowledgment of much more intense and often negative responses. Having recognized that intense responses do indeed exist in emotionally stable therapists, it became possible to examine such responses much more carefully and openly in the literature and at scientific meetings. Thus the door was opened to investigations of the potential usefulness, as well as the possible pitfalls, of such responses. Success in understanding the potential usefulness of countertransference responses, in turn, made further acknowledgment that much easier and that much more widespread. What we have referred to as the specifist movement in studies of countertransference appears to represent the inevitable outcome of such a progression, once set in motion.

In the chapters that follow, our efforts are very much in line with the general trajectory of current countertransference theory. In addition to examining countertransference phenomena from both a totalist and a specifist perspective, we shall present a schema for analyzing the therapist's identificatory experience. In so doing, we offer a theoretical integration of the concepts of empathy, projective identification, and countertransference by demonstrating that these phenomena, often thought to be disparate, are actually elements of one overall sequence through which a therapist can use his emotional responsiveness to achieve an empathic outcome.

3 *Discussion of Terms*

The experience of the therapist while he is in interaction with the patient plays a central role in the psychoanalytic understanding of the therapeutic process. The preceding chapter illustrated the historical progression from acknowledgment, through utilization, to the current specification of this essential ingredient in the therapy interaction. While every brand of psychoanalytically informed treatment acknowledges the therapist's experiential states, variations among distinct schools of clinical theory exist regarding how central a role the experience of the therapist plays in the therapeutic action of treatment and how much, if any, experiential information about the therapist ought to be included in the actual verbal exchange with the patient. Given its widespread recognition and its increasing utilization, surprisingly little has been written about the precise characteristics of this experiential process within the therapist.

What is the nature of the identificatory experience that underlies the phenomenon of countertransference? How can it be managed, understood, or processed so as to allow for a tolerable work environment for the therapist and also increase understanding of the patient and facilitate the therapeutic process? These questions of the "specifist" era can now be addressed as a consequence of the pioneering work examined in the previous chapter. The foundation of widespread acknowledgment of the therapist's experience allows us not only to recognize the existence of such experiences within the therapist, but also to investigate both the nature of their arousal and the sequences involved in their development and management.

Attempts to formulate understandings of these questions from the separate conceptual perspectives of empathy, projective identification, and countertransference have heretofore been preliminary and limited. Those authors who have been primarily interested in the phenomenon of empathy have examined the therapist's experience from the point of view of the impact of identifications on the therapist's ego functions. Those whose main interest has been the study of projective identification have concentrated on the projective and introjective mechanisms involved in the interactional transmission of an identification. Psychoanalytic investigators of countertransference have focused their attention on the technical utilization of the therapist's identifications from the vantage point of the consequent impairment or facilitation of the therapeutic process. Lacking is an integrated understanding of the therapist's experience, which unifies the three important conceptual perspectives. As stated in our introductory chapter, we believe that this important integration begins with the recognition that the concepts of empathy, projective identification, and countertransference represent aspects of one overall sequence for the processing of an identification. An integrated understanding of these three concepts must include a clear delineation of how the terms interface with one another, where they are distinct, where they are similar, and how these concepts bridge the intrapsychic versus interpersonal gap in psychoanalytic terminology.

As with any attempt to examine and integrate concepts that have different, sometimes even contradictory, meanings from one author to the next, precise definitions of key terms are essential. The present chapter is designed to define what we mean when we use certain terms and to elucidate the nature of their relationships to one another.

COUNTERTRANSFERENCE

As mentioned earlier, psychoanalytic examinations of the experience of the therapist have traditionally fallen under the heading of countertransference. Our definition of countertransference is consistent with that of the "totalist" perspective, whose shibboleth is that Freud's description of transference as "the greatest danger and the best tool for analytic work" (quoted in Racker, 1957, p. 303) may be applied with equal justification to countertransference, broadly defined as the therapist's total response to the patient, both conscious and unconscious. This "total response" includes all the thoughts and feelings that the therapist experiences in reaction to the therapeutic interaction whether they are considered to be "real" or "neurotically distorted." The totalist definition includes so-called objective countertransference reactions (Winnicott, 1949), which any therapist would likely experience in response to a patient in a particular context; it also includes what are considered to be the idiosyncratic reactions of the therapist arising from the therapist's own personal conflicts.

The totalist view of countertransference requires the therapist to direct what Freud (1912) called his "evenly suspended attention" not only to the patient, but also to the full range of his own thoughts and feelings, even if such thoughts and feelings at first blush seem irrelevant, inappropriate, or unacceptable. The therapist is encouraged to treat all thoughts and feelings as potentially important sources of information about the interaction with the patient. Within the totalist perspective on countertransference, the therapist, far from seeking to become impervious to the patient's influence, strives to appreciate the ways in which he is being *acted upon* by the patient. Sandler's (1976) notion of a "compromise" existing between the therapist's unique personality makeup and the patient's capacity to infuse the therapeutic relationship with his own particular wishes and needs is especially useful in assessing the degree of influence exerted by the therapeutic interaction upon the self experience of the therapist. We view countertransference as an umbrella term encompassing the concepts of projective identification, introjective identification, and empathy. Countertransference refers to all the reactions the therapist has in the interaction with the patient, reactions that may or may not be the result of projective identifications from the patient and may or may not be processed in a manner that could be labeled empathic. Empathic trial identifications (introjective identifications) are a subset of the larger universe of identificatory experiences existing under the label of countertransference. The interrelationships between the various subsets of countertransference will be explicated as we proceed through the definitions.

PROJECTIVE IDENTIFICATION

Several authors have made significant contributions to the development of the concept of projective identification. Klein (1946) introduced the term to refer to a child's *fantasy* of expelling bad parts of the self into the mother in order to rid the self of unwanted, aggressive aspects. According to the child's perception, these projected aspects of the self ultimately take control of the mother from within. Through this fantasy mechanism, the mother "is not felt to be separate but is felt to be the bad self" (p. 8). Thus the child establishes a continued sense of connection or identification with the projected part of the self. Kernberg (1975) maintained Klein's essentially intrapsychic framework in his definition of projective identification by viewing the mechanism as a pathological defensive operation in which the projection of aggression leads to specific circumscribed weaknesses of ego boundaries in the area of self-other differentiation and a need to control the external object arising from the fear of attack.

Malin and Grotstein (1966) examined the concept of projective identification in the context of the therapeutic process. While preserving Klein's (1946) definition of projective identification as an intrapsychic fantasy, they described the integral role played by projective identification, not only in the therapeutic process, but also in the overall development of ego integration:

> It seems to us that it is only upon perceiving how the external object receives our projection and deals with our projections that we now

> introject back into the psychic apparatus the original projection, but now modified on a newer level. The external object must confirm those constructive "good" aspects of the developing individual and thus facilitate higher ego integration which will mitigate the effect of the destructive components of the self [p. 28].

From this developmental perspective, Malin and Grotstein proposed that projective identification is a "normal, as well as abnormal, way of relating which persists into mature adulthood" (p. 27). Thc authors expanded the term projective identification by stating that, in addition to being a defense mechanism, it is also a way of establishing object relationships, which build ego integration throughout development; second, projective identification is an intrapsychic mechanism that sets in motion a *process* consisting of projective and introjective mechanisms, resulting in a "cycle" wherein projected aspects of self are re-introjected as a new "alloy" (p. 26). In a later valuable contribution, Grotstein (1981) explored the historical roots of projective identification, its relationship to the concept of splitting, and the central role it plays in the clinical setting.

It was Langs (1976) who vigorously addressed the interactional dimension of projective identification. He systematically analyzed the "interactional efforts" by both patient and therapist to induce in the other "aspects of his own inner state, so as to externally manage them and to evoke adaptive responses for reintrojection" (p. 277). Projective identification for Langs was the central element in the interactional field through which unconscious communications on the part of both coparticipants are transmitted.

Ogden's (1979, 1982) work on projective identification is extremely useful and illuminating in the clinical setting. Assimilating the contributions of several authors, he formulated a definition of projective identification that took into account the intrapsychic and interpersonal dimensions:

> The projector has the primarily unconscious fantasy of getting rid of an unwanted or endangered part of himself (including internal objects) and of depositing that part in another person in a powerfully controlling way. The projected part of the self is felt to be partially lost and to be inhabiting the other person. In association with this unconscious projective fantasy there is an interpersonal interaction by means

> of which the recipient is pursued to think, feel, and behave in a manner congruent with the ejected feelings and the self- and object-representations embodied in the projective fantasy [1982, p. 2].

Ogden's definition captures the sense of projective identification as an interactional process that serves the functions of communication, defensive operation, object relatedness, and a "pathway for psychological change." Like Kernberg (1975) but unlike Malin and Grotstein (1966), Ogden characterized projective identification as strictly pathological and indicative of "a primitive type of object relationship, a basic way of being with an object that is psychologically only partially separate" (p. 23).

Ogden's definition of projective identification as comprising three stages (inducement, metabolism, and reinternalization) broadens the term beyond the experience of the projector to include the reaction of an object and the eventual reintrojection of this reaction by the projector. We disagree with the breadth of Ogden's definition because there is much clarity to be gained by confining the term projective identification to the projector's experience of inducing a feeling state within an object. In contrast to Ogden, we maintain that the reaction of the object to this induced state, how well it is "metabolized" by the object, and the manner in which the projector "reinternalizes" what was initially projected are not aspects of projective identification. They respectively represent the distinct processes of: introjective identification on the part of the therapist, the empathic processing of that introjective identification by the therapist, and the introjective identification on the part of the projector. To subsume all of these separate processes under the name projective identification diminishes the precision of the term.

We define projective identification as a psychological operation with defensive, adaptive, and communicative properties. We agree with Malin and Grotstein (1966) that projective identification is a mechanism employed throughout development in an effort to promote ego integration and that its degree of primitivity or pathology varies widely according to the structural personality organization of the projector. Projective identification differs substantially from projection in that it exists only in the context of an interaction between two or more individuals, whereas projection is predominantly intrapsychic in nature and may or may not take place in an actual interpersonal relationship. Although having intrapsychic characteristics, projective identification represents an interactional phenomenon in which the projector, by actual influence, unconsciously elicits thoughts, feelings, and experiences within another individual which in some way resemble his own. In shorthand formulation, projection is to perception what projective identification is to influence. Hence we maintain that there can be no "successful" projective identification without a corresponding introjective identification on the part of the recipient of the projective identification. Our usage of the term goes beyond Klein's original, strictly intrapsychic view and conforms to what Sandler (1987) classifies as "second stage projective identification" (p. 17). The relationship between projective and introjective identification are described in the section defining introjective identification.

In projective identification, the projector may stir up within the therapist an experiential state that to some degree matches or complements the projector's immediate self experience. For example, a patient with sadomasochistic concerns who has consolidated a prevailing identification on the masochistic side may unconsciously communicate the enduring self-representation as victim by means of projective identification in one of three ways. First, he may elicit from the therapist, through actual interpersonal influence, an impulse to attack and criticize. The therapist would thus be pressured to identify his own immediate self-experience with the sadistic object representation of the patient, while the patient experiences his own enduring self-representation as victim.

Second, the predominantly masochistic patient may transiently assume the sadistic role as his immediate self-representation, thereby turning the tables so that the therapist feels attacked and criticized. In this instance, the therapist would be influenced to identify his own immediate self-experience as victim with the patient's enduring self-representation, now projected into the therapist, while the patient temporarily takes on the self-representation of sadist. Both the first and the second possibilities involving projective identification are what Racker (1957) describes as "complementary" identifications in which the therapist temporarily identifies with one aspect of the patient's internalized self- and object representational unit (introject), while the patient, at least temporarily, experiences the counterpart identification. The complementarity of the external interaction reflects the complementarity of the patient's internalized self- and object representational unit.

The third possibility, customarily associated with empathy, would result from the patient arousing within the therapist a "concordant" (Racker, 1957) identification such that, as mentioned earlier, the immediate self-experiences of both individuals are temporarily similar in nature. In this event, the therapist's momentary self-experience would provide him with a sense of harmonious understanding of his patient's enduring masochistic experience of victimization by someone or something outside of the therapeutic relationship. These three variations of a patient's projective identification and the therapist's corresponding introjective identification are specifically addressed in further detail under the definition of introjective identification (see Figure 1, p. 53).

We do not wish to imply by our broad view of projective identification that everything that goes on within the therapist in the interaction with the patient is a consequence of projective identification. The therapist's experience must reach a certain intensity of "self-quality" (Schafer, 1968) before it can be labeled an identification; likewise, there must be a significant degree of interactional pressure from the patient in order to label the therapist's introjective identification a direct response to the patient's projective identification. Many interactional communications are processed by the therapist without reaching the level of intensity necessary to be considered, by our definition, an introjective identification in response to a patient's projective identification.

The reception of a projective identification in the therapist is characterized by a temporarily heightened experience of self that is qualitatively different from the usual, more neutral experience of self-in-interaction with the patient. Once it can be determined that an identificatory experience has taken place within the therapist, it must then be decided to what degree this experience has been influenced by the interactional communications from the patient; that is to say, to what extent it has been projectively determined.

We concur with Sandler's (1976) conceptualization of the therapist's internal reactions to the patient as always involving "a compromise between his own tendencies or propensities and the role-relationship which the patient is unconsciously seeking to establish" (p. 47). Just as the therapist is not a blank screen, neither is he an empty container (Hoffman, 1983). Consequently, the introjective identification of the therapist never corresponds, point for point, with the projective identification sought by the patient. Deciding whether or not the therapist's heightened experience of himself is a consequence of a patient's projective identification must be the outcome of a validating process that occurs both in the silent formulation of an interpretation and in the assessment of the impact of an interpretation after it is posed. The subject of validation is taken up in greater detail in Chapter 8.

INTROJECTIVE IDENTIFICATION

In order to define adequately the term introjective identification one is faced with the additional task of defining several related complex terms. A clear understanding of introjective identification requires a similarly clear understanding of the following internalization processes: introjection, introject, identification, and identification with an introject.

The term introjection has both interactional and intrapsychic/structural components. Viewed in its interactional context, introjection refers to the taking in (introjecting) of what we have termed *interactional communications* from the therapeutic interaction. Interactional communication is a generic term for all communication, both in words and in action, that is transmitted consciously or unconsciously, through the interaction, by both patient and therapist. This taking in conforms to the classical definition of introjection outlined by Meissner (1972) and Kernberg (1976). In essence, there is a gradual buildup in

> the reproduction and fixation of an interaction with the environment by means of an organized cluster of memory traces implying at least three components: (i) the image of an object, (ii) the image of the self in interaction with that object, and (iii) the affective coloring of both the object image and the self image under the influence of the drive representative at the time of the interaction [Kernberg, 1976, p. 29].

The intrapsychic structural outcome of this continuous introjection process is an enduring, internal model (introject) of the self and the object in interaction. The introject, comprising self- and object representations, serves as a transitional phase of intrapsychic development between the reliance on external objects for self-regulation and the eventual autonomous regulatory ability that is achieved through the higher level internalization process of identification. Introjects achieve an intrapsychic "status" (Sandler and Rosenblatt, 1962 p. 138) within psychic organization capable of influencing drive regulation, ego functioning, and object relations (Meissner, 1972). Introjects provide internal models of self and objects that serve as the foundation for one's ultimate shaping of an enduring sense of self through the process of identification.

In the identification process, self-representations within the ego are modified "on the basis of another (usually an object) representation as a model" (Sandler and Rosenblatt, 1962, p. 137). The representations used as a model for identification are contained within introjects. The outcome for psychic structure resulting from this largely unconscious process is the collection of self-representations within the ego that form the building blocks for the core experience of self. Ego identity (Kernberg 1976), the highest level of internalization, represents a consolidation of these identifications into an enduring, organized sense of the self. We define self as the organization of component self-representations into a dynamic structure that provides the person with a continuous sense of "I." Identification, then, is the modification of enduring representations of self based on the influence of introjects. The process of identification assumes the modification of enduring self-representations modeled after aspects of either the self- or the object representations that make up the introject. Thus, all identifications are accomplished through identification with an introject.

This description of introjection, introjects, and identification is relatively straightforward and directly applicable to the usual course of developmental identifications. Is the same series of internalization processes, however, applicable for describing the temporary identifications the therapist experiences in the empathic process? Certainly empathic trial identifications are distinct, affectively tinged reactions that are experienced as having the same "self quality" (Schafer, 1968) as more enduring identifications. And yet these empathic identifications seem to be different from developmentally established identifications in their transient quality and the degree to which they permanently modify the sense of self. It is here that the concept of introjective identification can be useful in understanding the similarities and differences between these two distinct identification processes.

Although a good deal of study has been done on the separate processes of identification and introjection, relatively few authors (Klein, 1946, 1955; Langs, 1976; Malin and Grotstein, 1966; Grotstein, 1981) have discussed the actual mechanisms of introjective identification. Some authors (Meissner, 1980; Finnell 1986) feel the term is a confusing and counterproductive attempt to join two distinct aspects of the internalization process: identification and introjection. Again, our position is that the term introjective identification, if defined carefully, can clarify the intrapsychic and interpersonal elements involved in the temporary identification that the therapist experiences in response to a patient's projective identification.

We define introjective identification within the therapist as the reception of a projective identification from the patient. In order for a patient to engage in "successful" projective identification, there must be a corresponding introjective identification within the therapist. Conversely, introjective identification in the therapist can take place only in response to projective identification from the patient.

From a developmental perspective, introjective identification can be viewed as occupying a middle or transitional stage in the internalization sequence between introjection and identification. A clear understanding of introjective identification can be gained by breaking down the components of the term. "Introjective" refers to the fact that the introject being used for the identification is still actively under the "taking in," formation process. Viewed from the interpersonal perspective, the existence of the introject being used for identification purposes is still reliant on the interactional presence of an object. That is, introjective identification is an identificatory experience contingent on the interaction with the patient. It is an intrapsychic response (identification with an introject of the patient) that depends on the interactional pressure of the patient's projective identification. In other words, introjective identification involves the usual identification with an introject, but only in response to the interaction with an object. In the normal developmental sequence, identification with an introject can take place in the presence or absence of the significant object on whom the introject has been established. Introjective identification can take place only in the presence of an object and only in response to a projective identification from that object.

An example from a developmental context can illustrate the differences between identification with an introject and introjective identification. Two-year-olds begin to develop a sense of what they should or should not get into around the household. For the most part, parents are the models of this behavior-discrimination process by means of what they themselves do and by what they actively instruct children to do or not do. Children develop introjects of each parent coded with the instructions of right and wrong, as well as a multitude of other complex thoughts and feelings about the self in interaction with the parents. Children at this stage of actively learning the rules of the household will mature through a predictable sequence of internalization. At first, they know that a certain behavior is not allowed only by being in the presence of the parent and having the parent actively instruct them. Children progress along this self-regulatory sequence to the point where they can eventually recognize and even anticipate in the parents' absence which behaviors would likely elicit disapproval from the parents.

This elementary developmental example illustrates the two identification terms under discussion. The child who is dependent on the parents' presence for active guidance in this discrimination process can be said to engage in introjective identification (experience of following rules) in response to a clear projective identification (parents' exerting interactional pressure for rules to be followed) from the parents.[1] In the later

---

We acknowledge that this application of the term projective identification to a relatively common interaction represents a broader view of this concept than is held by those authors who restrict the definition of projective identification to a primitive, pathological defense mechanism. Our reasons for this broader perspective are contained in this chapter's discussion of projective identification.

stages of this sequence, the child who in the parents' absence is able to modify his or her behavior in accordance with the parents' dictates can be said to have identified with an introject of the parents. In this developmental light, introjective identification can be understood as a transitional phase in the internalization sequence during which introjects are in the process of being formed but have not yet achieved a more enduring psychic status.

Interactional Introject

The therapist's experience of projective identification is similar to that of the young child who is still actively forming the important introjects (representations of self in interaction with the parents) that will serve as a basis for self-guidance. The therapist also forms an internal model or introject of the patient-therapist relationship. We refer to the therapist's introject of the treatment process with each individual patient as the *interactional introject*.

This interactional introject has two components: a self- representation and an object representation. The self- representation is composed of all the experiences the therapist has had over time in the interaction with the patient. The object-representation component of this introject consists of impressions recorded by the therapist of the *patient's experience* of self, objects (both past and present), and the interaction with the therapist. From the moment he comes in contact with the patient, the therapist begins building his notion of what it is like for the patient to be himself, to experience various objects, and to relate to the therapist. This understanding of the therapist's internal model of the patient expands in several ways Greenson's (1960) notion of a "replica" of the patient (see Chapter 6). The internal object representation of the patient referred to here does not imply some objective recording of the patient's experience but rather the therapist's own perception of the patient's experience. The interactional introject is continuously being influenced and modified by the ongoing "taking in" of the experience of the therapeutic interaction.

When the therapist's immediate self-experience is identified with one of the two components (self- or object representation) of the interactional introject, his capacities to regulate and experience drive states, invoke ego operations, or engage in object relatedness are temporarily influenced. For example, a therapist experiences himself as unusually aggressive, sleepy, or hopeless with a certain patient but notes the absence of these self qualities in the interaction with the patient whose appointment follows immediately. This is a common occurrence and testifies to the "intrapsychic status" achieved by the interactional introject. Over time, the transient identificatory experiences established through the interactional introject can influence and shape more enduring identifications in the therapist's ego identity. The sum of the many patient-specific interactions will contribute to the development within the therapist of a "work ego"—an enduring representation of the self consolidated over time from the images of self in interaction with patients.

Figure 1 is a diagrammatic representation of the interactional introject. The diagram is arranged to present in parallel form the identificatory experiences of both the therapist and the patient. The projective identification of the patient is outlined on the left, and on the right is the outline for the corresponding introjective identification experienced by the therapist. First, few general points concerning this sketch. The experience of both patient and therapist is divided into two columns: immediate self-experience and introject. This categorization is meant to demonstrate how the identification with an aspect of the introject influences the person's immediate self-experience. The correspondences between the participants' identifications are classified as either concordant or complementary.

There are three combinations diagrammed for the matching of a patient's projective identification with a corresponding introjective identification on the part of the therapist. Reading from left to right under the first concordant variation, one begins with the experience of the patient. Here the patient's introject is composed of longstanding views of the self (self-representation) experienced as victim, and objects (object representation) experienced as victimizing. The self-representation aspect of this introject is the basis for an identification of the patient's immediate self-experience as victim. This immediate experience of self as victim is then communicated by the patient

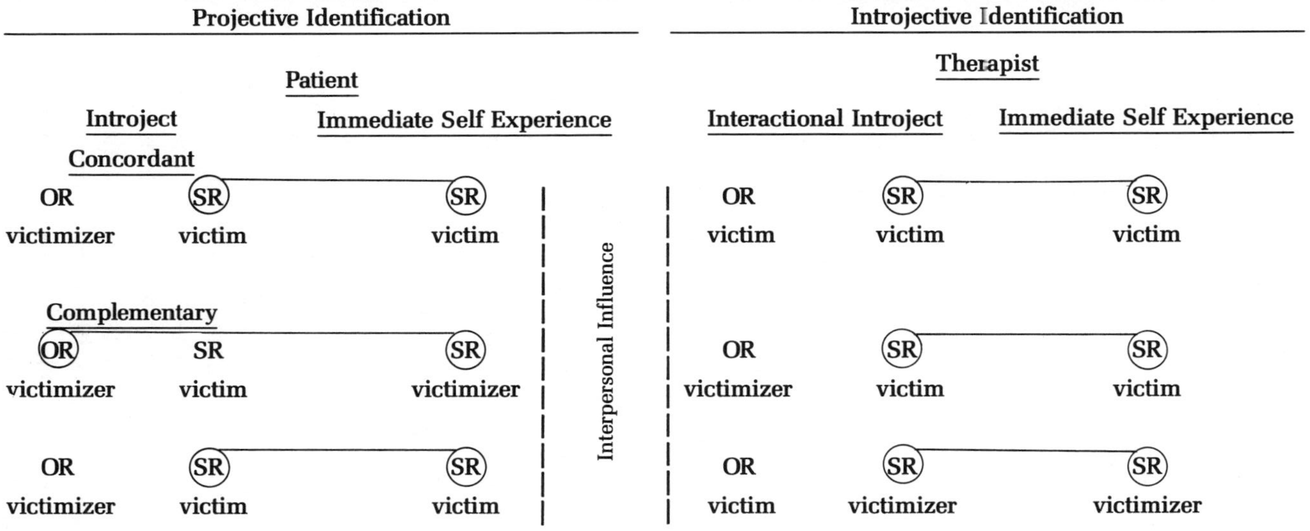

Projective Identification				Introjective Identification		
Patient				Therapist		
Introject		Immediate Self Experience		Interactional Introject		Immediate Self Experience
Concordant						
OR	(SR)	(SR)	Interpersonal Influence	OR	(SR)	(SR)
victimizer	victim	victim		victim	victim	victim
Complementary						
(OR)	SR	(SR)		OR	(SR)	(SR)
victimizer	victim	victimizer		victimizer	victim	victim
OR	(SR)	(SR)		OR	(SR)	(SR)
victimizer	victim	victim		victim	victimizer	victimizer

Key

SR = self representation

OR = object representation

SR–OR = Introject: A) For patient, enduring introjects of self and other paradigms
B) For therapist, interactional introject of self and patient interaction

Note: (i) Lines between circled representations indicate the identification with the aspect of the introject which is influencing each person's immediate self-experience.
(ii) Concordant and complementary are based on the matching or contrasting relationship between the immediate self-experience of each individual.

FIGURE 1

through the interpersonal process of projective identification to the therapist. The therapist receives this emotional transmission through his attentiveness to his own experience (self-representation) and his experience of the patient (object representation), both aspects of the interactional introject. In listening to and receiving the patient's interactional communications, the therapist experiences an emotional sense of what being a victim is like for the patient. The immediate self-experience of the therapist becomes identified with the object representation (patient's experience as victim) of the interactional introject. The correspondence between the patient's and the therapist's immediate self experience is concordant.

There are two forms of complementary arrangements. Under the first arrangement, the patient identifies his immediate self-experience with the object representation component of the introject, namely, the experience of object as victimizer. The patient takes on the role of victimizer and communicates this aggressive, domineering sense of himself to the therapist through the interaction. The therapist receives this communication experientially by feeling that he is the brunt of the patient's aggression and is occupying the uncomfortable role of victim. The therapist's interactional introject in this instance is registering the patient as victimizer and himself as victim. The immediate self-experience of the therapist then is identified with the self-representation (victim) component of the interactional introject. In this arrangement, the immediate self- experience of the patient as victimizer is complementary to the immediate self-experience of the therapist (victim).

The aforementioned complementary arrangement may be organized in a converse fashion. Simply, the patient may identify his immediate self-experience with the self-representation (victim) aspect of his introject. However, unlike either the complementary or concordant arrangements described earlier where the patient communicated to the therapist what the role of victim was like for the patient by inducing a state of victimization within the therapist, the patient under this particular complementary arrangement induces within the therapist a feeling of being a victimizer. Through the pressure of the interaction the patient manages to induce in the therapist thoughts, feelings, and wishes to be aggressive with the patient in a manner that conforms with the patient's experience of victimization from other objects. Again, the immediate self-experience of the patient (victim) is complementary to the immediate self-experience of the therapist (victimizer).

It is clear from the diagram that introjective identification is a process that the therapist undergoes in response to the patient's projective identification. The patient has several methods of communicating a projective identification and inducing a corresponding introjective identification within the therapist. However, the therapist also has a wide range of introjects derived from his own life experiences, and aspects (self- or object representations) of these introjects are potential models for identifications stimulated by the therapeutic interaction. As is discussed in a later chapter (see Validation, chapter 8), the therapist's identificatory experiences with the patient, based primarily on the evocation of introjects established independently of the treatment process, must be scrutinized closely for their degree of plausible correspondence to the patient's immediate self-experience. This is an area in which the therapist's awareness of self is vital.

For example, a therapist may listen to a patient grieve over the loss of a loved one. During this listening process the therapist may begin to feel some of the patient's sense of sadness and recall a time in his own experience when he himself lost someone very significant. The situation of the loss may be recalled in detail—the people who lent support, the sense of sadness and hopelessness, and so on. The therapist may feel quite sad as he briefly relives his own experience of loss in reaction to the patient's material. The therapist in this circumstance is certainly undergoing an identificatory experience. The therapist's immediate self-experience of sadness, however, is not *solely* a result of the influence of the interactional introject. The stimulation of the patient's presentation of grief has evoked an introject within the therapist that was formed long ago, apart from the present therapeutic relationship. In this instance the therapist may be considered to have experienced a concordant introjective identification influenced by the interactional introject (sadness), which has further stimulated an identification with the introject (influence of separate long-standing introject).

Complex as this example may seem, the associations retrieved by the therapist through this identification with an introject can provide rich insights to shed light on parallel experiences of the patient. The therapist in the previous example, for instance, might, under the affective pressure of the patient's story find himself aware of particular associations to his own past experience of loss. Having pulled back from the emotional sway of this identificatory experience, he might recognize that the sense of helplessness evoked by his own associations bears a striking resemblance to a similar but unacknowledged experience suggested by the patient's material.

THE EMPATHIC PROCESS VIS-À-VIS COMPLEMENTARY IDENTIFICATIONS

Empathy has been defined as "the inner experience of sharing in and comprehending the momentary psychological state of another person" (Schafer, 1959, p. 345). In shorthand formulations, it has been referred to as "vicarious introspection" (Kohut, 1959, p. 459) and "emotional knowing" (Greenson, 1960, p. 418). It is widely agreed that empathy is characterized by two components accompanied by varying degrees of awareness in the therapist, which unfold across a spectrum of time, ranging from the instantaneous "flash" of understanding to the more gradual crystallizations garnered over many sessions.

The first component of empathy is what Fliess (1942) referred to as the therapist's "trial identification" with his patient. This identification requires a receptivity and openness on the part of the therapist, who actively seeks and welcomes this transitory introjective identification just as the theater audience is eager to be stimulated and moved by the players. The traditional view of the empathic trial identification corresponds to what Racker (1957) termed a "concordant identification," in which the transitory self-experience of the therapist closely matches the patient's self-representation at that particular moment. The empathic experience, again as it is traditionally defined, is characterized in the therapist by feelings of harmony and closeness with his patient, as well as by the experience of positive self-regard for performing a job well.

The second component of empathy concerns the oscillation within the therapist's "work ego" (Fliess, 1942) from the "free play of fantasy to critical scrutiny" (Ferenczi, 1919, p. 178). Beres and Arlow (1974) described a shift from thinking and feeling with the patient to thinking about the patient, and Schafer (1959) referred to a movement from the experiencing ego to the observing ego.

The "creative regression" in the therapist, which is necessary for the empathic trial identification to be aroused, remains controlled and temporary. The feelings associated with the therapist's trial identification may then be hypothesized by the therapist to represent "signal affects" (Schafer, 1959; Zetzel, 1965; Olinick, 1969; Beres and Arlow, 1974), which alert him to the inner experience of his patient.

We emphasize that the foregoing is the traditional view of empathy, because we believe that it is both incomplete and misleading. We will demonstrate throughout this volume that the empathic trial identification is not limited to concordant identifications, but may also entail a "complementary identification" (Deutsch, 1926; Racker, 1957), in which the therapist's momentary experience of self closely matches the patient's internalized object representation at a given moment in time. The empathic trial identification need not entail an initial concordant identification for an empathic outcome to occur. Similarly, a concordant identification does not always eventuate in an empathic outcome.

We believe that Racker's (1957) concept of concordant identification is no more synonymous with the usual meaning of empathy than is complementary identification. Concordant and complementary identifications represent "trial identifications" (Fliess, 1942) that a therapist utilizes in his pursuit of an empathic understanding of the patient's experience. To define empathy as synonymous with concordant identification does not adequately address clinical phenomena. Are we to say that the therapist who is overwhelmed by a powerful concordant identification with a hopeless patient has achieved an empathic understanding of this patient? We are all familiar with instances of concordant identifications leading not to empathy, but to countertransference turmoil. The therapist who becomes swamped in his patient's feelings of hopelessness nevertheless has the potential for reaching an empathic outcome if the powerful concordant trial identification is successfully processed through the subphases we will outline. *It is our contention that the potential for an empathic outcome also lies in the successful processing of complementary identifications.*

We are not proposing that these two forms of identification (concordant and complementary) on the therapist's part should be conceptualized *as* empathy, but rather that they are forms of introjective identification that may ultimately lead to an empathic outcome. Empathy is the optimal outcome that results from the successful processing of an identification and leads to emotional knowledge of the patient's experience. Empathy is a process, not just an identification. In building on the traditional view of empathy as a two-step process, we are extending the usual conceptualization of empathy to include complementary as well as concordant identifications in the empathic process. To limit empathic identifications only to the concordant variety, as has been traditionally held, simply does not hold up in an analysis of the therapist's experience of the therapeutic process. We are widening the definition of empathy from an intrapsychic event involving only concordant identifications taking place within the therapist—either with or without the patient's influence—to an interpersonal process in which a series of steps leads to an empathic outcome in the therapist's understanding of the patient.

The argument can be made that empathy involves only concordant identifications since empathy requires the therapist's experiential state to resemble the patient's experiential state at the moment of communicative interaction. An objection can be raised to the inclusion of complementary identifications in a definition of the empathic process because complementary identifications, by definition, involve the therapist's experiencing an emotional state that is complementary—and often highly adversarial—to the patient's experience at the moment of communication. Again, this argument denotes a static and narrow view of empathy. While it is true that during the moment of communication in a complementary identification the therapist is not experiencing feelings concordant with those of his patient, there is nevertheless an important emotional correspondence between the two participants' experiential states.

If one conceptualizes empathy as a process—not as a static identification—then this process can be said to include a complementary identification optimally leading to a concordant identification. The therapist who processes a complementary identification in the manner we will describe later ultimately may gain a concordant emotional knowledge of the patient's experience. The initial complementary identification serves as a vehicle for an eventual concordant identification within the therapist.

For example, a therapist may be able to validate satisfactorily (see chapter 8) that his uncharacteristic feelings of profound inadequacy in working with a particular patient are largely a consequence of interactional pressure from the patient. He then has the opportunity to make use of this insight both to learn a great deal about the patient's experiential state and to know what it is like to be in the patient's shoes. It is a *relationship* that the patient has helped to bring to life (the therapist, of course, contributes also) in the therapeutic interaction; it does not go far enough to say that the patient has merely engendered complementary feelings within the therapist. This relationship likely reflects other relationships for the patient, past and present, in which one participant, for whatever reasons, needs to pressure another into a sense of profound inadequacy. As in all interpersonal paradigms, two persons are involved, and it is usually the case that the patient has been both on the giving and the receiving end of this kind of attack, subtle or not so subtle, on adequacy. That the patient is probably familiar with both sides of whatever interpersonal paradigm is constructed in the therapeutic interaction also constitutes a persuasive argument for the inclusion of complementary identification in the empathic process. In the processing of a complementary identification, not only does the therapist have an avenue for understanding his counterpart in the interaction by beginning with an exploration of his own feelings, but what the therapist is experiencing at a particular moment may very well be something the patient himself has experienced. The patient, for example, may be familiar with both the role of attacker and the role of victim.

Our inclusion of complementary identifications in the empathic process represents an *extension* of—rather than a radical departure from—existing psychoanalytic theory on the subject of empathy. Although a very small minority of those who have written on this subject, others (Deutsch, 1926; Beres and Arlow, 1974; Langs, 1976) have alluded to this position without seeming to develop the fullest implications of their conceptualizations, as the following excerpt clearly illustrates (Beres and Arlow, 1974):

> The affect which the therapist experiences may correspond precisely to the mood which the patient has sought to stimulate in him as, for example, a masochist who tries to evoke criticism and attack. Empathy in such instances consists of recognizing that this is precisely what the patient wishes to provoke in the analyst. The affect experienced is a signal affect alerting the therapist to the patient's motivation and fantasy. If the therapist does not recognize this, then empathy has failed and countertransference takes over [p. 35].

These authors are stating that a complementary identification, (although they do not use the term) can play a very important role in the empathic process. It is unfortunate that they do not ever develop this point beyond what is contained in these sentences. The presentation of our schema (chapters 4–7) elaborates our view that complementary identifications are to be included in an understanding of the empathic process.

THE RELATIONSHIP BETWEEN EMPATHY AND PROJECTIVE IDENTIFICATION

The operations of empathy and projective identification have traditionally been differentiated with respect to four characteristics: the intense versus mild impact on the therapist, the intrapsychic versus interpersonal nature of the process; pathology versus normality; and the therapist's degree of conscious control over versus unconscious reactiveness to the experience.

Empathy is universally regarded as a welcomed identificatory experience on the part of the therapist. The patient's communications are usually viewed as being conveyed in a nondemanding manner, actively sought after and received by the therapist, and syntonically integrated into the therapist'sself experience. The therapist is seen as maintaining a degree of conscious control over this experience, marked by appropriate therapeutic objectivity and distance. The patient is viewed as engaging in a normal, noncoercive, predominantly verbal method of communication that employs subtle, well-modulated channels of transmission in the interaction between participants. Self- and object boundaries are described as well differentiated.

In sharp contrast, the therapist as object of a patient's projective identification tends to be viewed as having to struggle more or less passively to cope with any of an array of intensely uncomfortable self-experiences evoked by the forceful pull of the interaction with the patient. He is frequently seen as having lost necessary objectivity and distance from his own experience largely because of the less conscious nature of the aroused self-experience and the unacceptability of the associated affect. The patient is viewed as engaging in a pathological, coercive, largely nonverbal, "primitive" method of communication that employs unavoidably intrusive modes of transmission. Self- and object boundaries are described as poorly differentiated.

These characterizations tend to obfuscate the interrelationship more than they clarify the distinction between empathy and projective identification. Although previous authors (Grinberg, 1962; Segal, 1964; Langs, 1976; Ogden, 1982; Sandler, 1987) have touched on the subject, the manner in which empathy and projective identification are related has not been examined in sufficient depth.

Consider the following two examples. First, a patient arrives for his session and begins to sob over the sudden death of a beloved pet on whom he has relied for several years as a companion. In response, the therapist notes in himself a growing feeling of sadness and a suppressed impulse to cry. Second, a patient begins the session with a scathing criticism of the therapist's office decor, noting with sarcasm the lack of sophistication in various paintings and the incongruence between types of furniture. Under the continuous pressure of this criticism, the therapist recalls the time when he selected his office furnishings and remembers his feelings of inadequacy in coordinating various pieces. His reawakened sense of incompetence grows as the patient's critical eye moves from one item in the office to another. The therapist's experience gradually shifts to a feeling of anger toward the patient.

The first example is illustrative of what is commonly viewed as an empathic trial identification, whereas the second example is prototypical of the therapist as recipient of a patient's projective identification. The therapist's introjective identification is concordant in the first example and complementary in the second. These distinctions obscure the two-fold relationship between empathy and projective identification.

First, we propose that in the process of a therapist's achieving empathic contact with his patient, some degree of projective identification from the patient is virtually always involved, whether mild or intense in quality. In the first example, the lump in the therapist's throat did not occur in a vacuum, nor does any empathic trial identification (whether concordant or complementary) spring full-blown in the mind of a therapist. In addition to the therapist's receptivity, the achievement of empathic contact always involves the interpersonal "sending power" of the patient such that the induced trial identification is the outcome of a radically mutual interactive process between patient and therapist in which the therapist receives and processes projective identification from the patient.

In both examples, the therapist was stimulated and influenced by the patient to feel as he felt. There is neither more nor less coerciveness in either example. Both therapist reactions are interpersonally stimulated and involve strong emotions for the therapist that could potentially lead to a clearer understanding of the patient's internal world. The second example may or may not have been more "intense" for the therapist, but intensity alone in no way justifies a dichotomization between the processes of empathy and projective identification. We do not believe that it is useful to think of one as normal and the other as pathological. Both examples depict a powerful form of emotional communication that opens up for the therapist an avenue of understanding that is "beyond words" (Grotstein 1981, p. 202).

There is a second aspect to the relationship between empathy and projective identification. *Whereas in empathy, projective identification is virtually always involved, we believe that in a therapist's handling of a patient's projective identification, there is always the potential for an empathic outcome, whether*

or not this potential is actualized. In the second clinical example, the therapist has the opportunity to pull back from the induced countertransference experience in order to consider why it might be that the patient needs him to feel as he is feeling. In so doing, the door is opened to vivid emotional insight about the patient. Projective identification is often at the root of therapeutic impasses, failed treatments, stormy countertransference reactions, and various other forms of empathic derailment. In such cases, the therapist in some way or another often comes to view his self-experience as a concrete "reality" rather than as a powerful source of understanding regarding both what is happening in the therapeutic interaction and why the patient may need him to feel this way. Although Schafer (1983, p. 76) does not use the term projective identification, we believe it is this phenomenon that he is describing when he speaks of a patient's "attacks on empathizing." A patient's projective identification *may* indeed lead to a coercive provocation of the therapist and result in what is often a destructive reenactment of past interpersonal trauma for the patient. But it may not have to be so.

In both those brief examples there is an "induced" feeling state in the therapist aroused by the patient's interactional communications. This induced feeling state signals a trial identification that represents the culmination of the first phase of the empathic sequence we outline in this volume. By scrutinizing this trial identification, the therapist gains access to a set of meanings that lays the groundwork for true emotional knowledge of the patient. The typical examples associated with projective identification may very well involve a high degree of pressure from the patient, considerable discomfort for the therapist, and difficulty in stepping back to examine and process. But when this containment and processing of the projective identification does occur, it paves the way for an empathic outcome. There is a fundamental sameness between what is typically referred to as the processing of a projective identification and the objective scrutiny of an empathic trial identification.

In attempting to examine how a patient communicates with a therapist and influences him to respond in one way or another, the decision about the degree of coerciveness, disruptiveness, intensity, or psychopathology involved is essentially arbitrary. We have concluded that much is to be gained from recognizing the commonality between the easily, quickly, and preconsciously processed "flash" experience of empathy and the much more difficult, as times even tumultuous, processing of an exceedingly uncomfortable projective identification that involves considerable time and conscious energy. The following chapters present a clinical schema that illuminates the commonality to which we refer.

4 The Unitary Sequence for Processing Interactional Communications

An Introduction

We have discussed the fact that empathy and projective identification have generally been viewed as unrelated—if not thoroughly antipathetic—clinical phenomena, with the former traditionally associated with a harmonious transference-countertransference paradigm and the latter typically mentioned in connection with countertransference turmoil and loss of perspective. Working within the tradition that views psychoanalytic therapy as a radically mutual process and that considers countertransference (broadly defined as the therapist's total response to the patient) as a potentially useful tool, we have proposed (Burke and Tansey, 1985; Tansey and Burke, 1985) that empathy and projective identification represent interrelated aspects of a unitary sequence for the therapist's processing of interactional communications from the patient. Drawing upon and extending the work of previous authors (Fliess, 1942, 1953; Greenson, 1960; Olinick, 1969) who have discussed sequences related to empathy, as well as those who have examined stages of internal events occurring in the therapist in relation to projective identification (Malin and Grotstein, 1966; Ogden, 1979, 1982) we have outlined a sequence consisting of three phases: Reception, Internal Processing, and Communication. In the first phase, the therapist receives the patient's interactional communications and is thereby acted upon and influenced by the patient; the second phase encompasses the therapist's internal experience and analysis of what has been communicated through the interaction by the patient; and the final phase entails the therapist "giving back" to the patient through the interaction what has been internally processed.

The three phases and their respective subphases are outlined according to the temporal sequence of the therapist's experience during the processing of an interactional communication. The schema, however, *is not a cookbook formula*. Although the phases are presented in a particular order and the movement within any phase corresponds to the degree of processing of the interactional communication by the therapist, the sequence of processing involves a great deal of dynamic interplay between phases and subphases. In other words, the schema is based on an overall temporal sequence that always applies, but within which there is variation and flexibility. This point will become clearer in the material to follow.

At any particular moment in time, the processing of an interactional communication by the therapist may be assessed with regard to what has been accomplished in any or all of the three phases. Although the preponderance of the therapist's efforts may momentarily lie in any one of the three phases, almost always some work is being done in all three phases simultaneously. As the therapist moves forward from one phase to the next, the processing involved in the prior phase or subphase continues; hence, progress within any phase or subphase continuously enhances and builds upon the work accomplished in all preceding phases or subphases. Similarly, problems along the way may erode what has been accomplished in prior subphases. In this way, the therapist's actual experience of the overall processing sequence is fluid and dynamic rather than rigidly defined by the movement from one completed phase or subphase to the next in a mechanical, rote manner. In this regard, we share Greenson's (1960) view concerning the difficulties inherent in describing the various events that occur in a fluid process:

> one has to magnify the intervals and separate steps in an occurrence in which much seems to happen very rapidly and perhaps simultaneously . . . . The steps do not go in a straight sequence, but there are oscillations and variations and simultaneous occurrences [p. 421, 422].

The sequence of phases for processing interactional communications outlined in the following chapters assumes that the therapist is operating within the broad spectrum of psychoanalytic psychotherapy, with an awareness that transference and countertransference issues are essential elements in the therapeutic process. Within the psychoanalytic spectrum, there are several schools of thought, each of which emphasizes its own formulation of intrapsychic events and their interpersonal correlates. Such distinctions are usually accompanied by differences in the technical application of this knowledge within the therapeutic exchange. For instance, opinions vary as to the relative emphasis placed on genetic material, the here-and-now interaction, the transference, and current extratransference material. Similarly, countertransference disclosure is encouraged in some quarters and virtually forbidden in others. Irrespective of the extent to which one emphasizes interpretations dealing primarily with immediate transference material as opposed to genetic or current extransference material, if a therapist has a clearer understanding of what he is experiencing and how that might be useful rather than disruptive, he is in a much better position to implement whatever technique he happens to favor. The same is true regardless of his position on countertransference disclosure. The schema offers a framework that facilitates the therapist's understanding of his internal reactions and helps lay the groundwork for the ultimate technical application of the emotional knowledge of the patient that has been achieved.

The therapist's capacity to entertain various trial identification is correlated with his tolerance for what may be difficult self-experiences. This capacity is critical in the achievement of an empathic outcome. A corollary of this important relationship is that the therapist's degree of conscious awareness of his internal state at any point in the processing sequence depends largely on his capacity to tolerate the image of self that is aroused by the interactional communication from the patient.

Optimally, the therapist is a willing recipient of the introjective identifications that are induced by the patient's interactional pressure. However, therapists differ in their willingness to tolerate potentially uncomfortable self-states, depending on the particular dynamic involved and the intensity with which it is transmitted. The therapist, for example, who is being portrayed relentlessly by his patient as withholding, incompetent, intentionally depriving, and greedy is truly on the "hot seat." Although there certainly are occasions when a therapist must impose limits on a patient's actions, it is the ability to tolerate and become aware of the powerful feelings stirred up by such forceful interactional communications that largely determines a therapist's progress within the sequence of phases described in the following chapters.

A disruption in the empathic process is defined as a difficulty in any subphase that prevents or impedes further processing of a patient's projective identification toward an empathic outcome. The duration and severity of the disruption depends largely on the strength of the patient's projective identification relative to the therapist's capacity to tolerate the experience of self associated with the reception of the projective identification.

Borrowing from the developmental literature, we have delineated two general patterns of empathic disruption—arrest and regression—which may occur at any subphase level in the Reception and Internal Processing phases. They differ in the impact of the disturbance on the empathic processing sequence. Empathic arrest refers to a breakdown in the therapist's empathic work at a particular subphase level such that, although he is unable to proceed further in the processing sequence, he is nevertheless able to continue successfully managing the work of the previous subphases leading up to the disturbance. This clinical scenario is parallel to what occurs in a developmental arrest.

Empathic regression, on the other hand, refers to a breakdown at a particular point in the empathic process that is severe enough to disrupt the therapist's management of earlier subphases. The extent of the empathic regression—that is, how many earlier subphases are negatively affected by the breakdown—will vary according to the extent of the therapist's discomfort with the particular projective identification being processed. The greater the severity of the impact of a disturbance at a specific subphase level, the greater will be the regressive influence on prior subphases.

Disruptions occurring throughout the processing sequence vary with the amount of emotional knowledge the therapist has been able to gain about the patient. The location of the disruption within the processing sequence does not necessarily reflect the degree of severity of the empathic disturbance. Any of the disruptions described might eventuate in severe consequences for the empathic process, regardless of where they occur in the sequence.

The following chapters present a subphase-by-subphase examination of the sequence for processing interactional communications. The discussion of each subphase includes a definition of the therapeutic task facing the therapist; a description of potential adaptations on the part of the therapist ranging from optimal to disrupted management of the subphase task; and lastly, clinical examples illustrating both optimal and disrupted processing as well as communications from therapist to patient that signal the status of the therapist's progress in the processing sequence. A separate chapter is devoted to each of the three phases of Reception, Internal Processing, and Communications.

5 *The Reception Phase*

The Reception phase is the first of three stages in the empathic processing of interactional communications. It consists of three hierarchically arranged subphases through which the therapist must advance in order to receive and experience the particular sense of self aroused by the patient's projective identification. Disruptions in any of the three subphases of Reception may result in an empathic arrest such that the therapist is unable to move ahead into Internal Processing. This arrest is accompanied by a verbal or nonverbal communication to the patient that conveys the specific breakdown in the empathic process. Furthermore, problems that may subsequently arise in either the Internal Processing or the Communication phases can result in a regressive unravelling of the previously intact achievements of the Reception phase in any or all of its three subphases. Thus, we reiterate the critical point that although the Reception phase is the starting point of the processing sequence, its therapeutic tasks remain ongoing throughout the entire process. At any point a therapist may falter in his or her interactional receptivity for reasons that our schema will help to illuminate.

SUBPHASE 1. MENTAL SET

This subphase initiates the empathic process. The term mental set refers to the therapist's mental activity immediately before and during the session with a particular patient. The therapist aspires to a state of mind characterized by the absence of preoccupation with outside matters and allowing for optimal attention to the interactional presence of the patient. What is called for here is not a deliberate effort to concentrate, but rather what Freud (1912) referred to as "evenly suspended attention," in which the therapist does not direct his "notice to anything in particular." It should be added that, for the most part, Freud referred to evenly suspended attention to everything concerning the patient while the therapist puts his own feelings aside. In stating that the therapist "should simply listen, and not bother about whether he is keeping anything in mind" (p. 112), Freud believed he was prescribing the "necessary counterpart" to the recommendation that the patient free associate.

Spence (1982) refuted Freud's position that the therapist's evenly hovering attention represents the complement to the patient's free association. He suggested that free-floating listening can occur only when the patient is presenting "a fully controlled piece of exposition" (p. 115) in contrast to "the usual kind of fragmentary utterances" that occur the bulk of the time, the latter requiring of the therapist a more active style of listening. We agree with Spence, in part, in that a therapist's listening stance can never be entirely free from any of a multitude of influences—theoretical biases, associations triggered by the patient's presentation, how the day is going, particular concerns about the patient or hypotheses as to the meaning of his communications, and so on—all of which may be said to interfere with truly evenly hovering attention. The same point has been made with respect to "free association," in that a patient's "utterances" are never entirely devoid of censorship, conscious or unconscious. Similarly, a therapist can never be said to be entirely neutral in his presentation to the patient, though he may exercise restraint so as to allow the patient maximum opportunity to construe what he believes the analyst's position to be.

Everyone familiar with psychological testing understands the effortful concentration required to perform well on the Arithmetic subtest. This mental facility is quite different from the free-flowing, spontaneous attention necessary to perform well on Digit Span, a subtest calling for the subject to repeat an increasingly long series of numbers orally presented by the examiner. The latter state of mind represents the optimal listening stance during the first stage of the empathic process, when the therapist is seeking heightened receptivity to an empathic trial identification. In contrast to Spence, we believe that to the extent that the therapist is able to achieve evenly hovering attention, he is optimally prepared to be influenced by the patient, by the interaction, and by cues coming from within. As we explore in the subphases to follow, evenly hovering attention will of course have to give way to a more concentrated, effortful "search after meaning" (Spence, 1982, p. 107) especially at that point when the therapist recognizes signal affects emanating from within.

In describing this same process, Sandler (1976) spoke of the need for "free-floating attention" by which the therapist simultaneously allows "all sorts of thoughts, day-dreams and associations to enter consciousness while he is at the same time listening to and observing the patient" (p. 44). Sandler was suggesting that Freud's evenly suspended attention should be directed not only to the patient but also to the therapist's own material emanating from within. But in addition Sandler elaborated Freud's recommendation still further by advocating what he called "free-floating responsiveness" in the therapist. He proposed that a therapist's experience with a particular patient most often represents a *compromise* between his own tendencies or propensities and the role-relationship the patient is unconsciously seeking to establish. Thus, by focusing free-floating attention not only on thoughts, feelings, and associations coming from within, but also on his own overt *behavior*, the analyst may learn something very important about the patient in light of the roles the patient may unconsciously be seeking to orchestrate. Within the limits established by the treatment situation, free-floating responsiveness in actions—such as the use of humor or the particular way the patient is greeted—can thus be a potentially useful source of empathic insight.

There appear to be two categories of disruption in the therapist's initial establishment and ongoing maintenance of an optimal mental set. The first can be described as characterological, resulting from ongoing, unresolved conflicts and concerns within the therapist's own personality makeup. Whether or not the patient consciously perceives it, a therapist's characterological disruptions may be manifested in such phenomena as enduring blind spots, rigidity, aloofness, hypersensitivity or insensitivity to certain issues, prejudicial stereotyping, chronic anxiousness, arrogance, timidity, and the like, all of which interfere with listening. In this context, Schafer's (1983, p. 44) point deserves mentioning that a therapist may, for example, seem timid or inconsiderate in social settings and yet have no trace of this interference with the "second self" he presents in the treatment situation.

Characterological disruptions often pose a severe and lasting impediment to the therapist's capacity to receive particular projective identifications from a patient. Whereas a specific characterological disruption for a therapist may interfere with one patient, it may not be detectable in the treatment of another because the latter patient does not pull strongly for this disrupted response from the therapist. For instance, a therapist who has a characterological need for order and tight control over the flow of events may refuse a patient's request to reschedule an appointment. The therapist may justify his refusal on the grounds of "preserving the therapeutic frame" and interpret the patient's resistance to treatment. If in fact the patient's request is reasonable and in good faith, a derailment of the empathic process will have occurred. This same therapist might not have a problem with a second patient, who feels the same need for absolute orderliness as the therapist, though in this case it is hard to imagine the therapist's difficulty not surfacing in some other variation.

The psychoanalytic literature is replete with examples of what we would categorize as disruptions in mental set. At times, the examples are portrayed as strictly intrapsychic events unfolding within the therapist and having nothing to do with the patient; other illustrations do take into account the interactional presence of the patient. We propose that except in those extreme situations in which the therapist is either very poorly trained or altogether unsuited for clinical work, it is always useful to maintain an interactional focus and to consider possible ways in which the patient may have stimulated the therapist's response. Even if the contribution of the patient is felt to be slight, this awareness may nevertheless prove to be very useful to the therapist, both in overcoming the disruption and in learning something about himself and the patient. Even the therapist who refuses to reschedule appointments may find himself feeling either more or less inclined to be flexible with a given patient.

It goes without saying that all therapists work well with certain types of patients and less well, or even poorly, with others. Although generalizations regarding working with "types" of patients can be unproductive and misleading, at the outset of treatment it is often the gross characteristics of the patient that elicit characterological disruptions in mental set for the therapist. What if the patient is a strikingly attractive member of the same or opposite sex; young or old; wealthy, middle class or poor, intellectualized or emotionally expressive; physically large or small; caucasian or minority?

To illustrate a characterological disruption in mental set, let us take the case of a young therapist who tended to feel inadequate. Despite having made good progress in working through this concern in her own treatment and despite having demonstrated real talent as a therapist, she nevertheless remained vulnerable to excessive self-doubt in the face of certain countertransference pressures. This therapist was referred a patient by a former supervisor whom she highly respected. The referral patient was the wife of a current patient of the former supervisor. Although initially pleased by the referral, the therapist began to dwell on the fact that the former supervisor would have the opportunity to evaluate her work on a regular, ongoing basis because of his own work with the husband. Thus, before even meeting with the patient, the therapist experienced a recrudescence of anxiety and feelings of self-doubt aroused by the fear of disappointing the former supervisor, whose opinion meant a great deal to her.

In the initial interview, the patient presented with a great deal of skepticism as to the potential value of psychotherapy, thus exacerbating the therapist's preexisting problems in mental set. The patient sensed the therapist's timidity and lack of self-assurance and did not return for a second session. The combination of factors—characterological tendency to self-doubt, fear of disappointing a respected colleague, defensive skepticism from the patient—so riddled the therapist's capacity for free-floating attention and responsiveness that the empathic process was subtly but abruptly short-circuited even before the interactional pressure from the patient could be developed more fully. Because the patient was reflecting the therapist's own personal concerns, the therapist responded to the patient's skepticism in a way that subtly verified the patient's concerns. Had this patient been referred by someone else, the therapist might have had better success in managing her own tendencies toward self-doubt.

A second class of disruptions in mental set can be understood as situational, referring to a therapist's inability to attend adequately as a consequence of transitory concerns. Lack of sleep, overwork, and personal crises are common examples of situational intrusions upon a therapist's mental set. Major life events, such as marriage or the birth of a child, may also interfere. Similarly, disruptions may result from preoccupation with previous or upcoming appointments that are unusually stressful for one reason or another. A therapist may also become preoccupied by previous sessions with the same patient such that feelings of apprehension, guilt, or excitement erode his mental set and derail the empathic process. Situational disruptions, as long as they remain temporary and do not set in as chronic patterns, are less severe than characterological disruptions. Uncharacteristic or transitory distractibility, irritability, impatience, boredom, overenthusiasm, unusual humorousness or humorlessness, not hearing or forgetting what a patient has said, answering phone calls during sessions, and lateness for appointments are common examples of ways in which situational disruptions can be communicated. Given our interactional emphasis, however, it remains important to consider the patient's potential contribution. For example, a therapist in the midst of a situational crisis may find it more difficult to attend with one patient than with another, reflecting what might be varying abilities to elicit attention from one patient to the next.

A clinical example of a situational disruption in mental set might involve a therapist who received a telephone call from a current patient in an acute crisis just prior to the beginning of a session with another patient. During the beginning segment of this session, the therapist found himself preoccupied with thoughts about the clinical condition of the patient in crisis such that he was unable to attend adequately to the patient before him. He communicated this to the patient by a sense of distance evinced by less verbal activity. The patient may or may not consciously have noticed or been able to convey to the therapist this sense of difference in the quality of his presence with the patient. At such times, the therapist would have been less capable of receiving the interactional communications being transmitted by the patient, and the empathic process would have been temporarily disrupted at this subphase.

SUBPHASE 2. INTERACTIONAL PRESSURE

In this subphase, the therapist begins to experience the emotional pressure of the patient's interactional communication. Within the limits of his or her tolerance, it is the therapist's task to allow the patient the freedom to develop the communication through the verbal and nonverbal channels of the therapeutic interaction. In so doing, the therapist is required to sustain an openness to being influenced emotionally by the patient in order to be receptive to the induction of a projective identification.

Disruptions at this juncture of the empathic process typically fall into one of two opposite categories. At one extreme, the therapist assumes an overly rigid or controlling posture, thereby consciously or unconsciously shutting off or clamping down on the interactional transmission of a patient's projective identification in its incipient stage before the identification has really taken hold within the therapist. Such breakdowns appear to occur as a consequence of the potency of the patient's communication and his style and form of transmitting that communication relative to the therapist's tolerance and reactive potential to these elements. The therapist refuses to allow himself to be emotionally influenced or acted upon further by the patient. He is not aware of the meaning of what the patient is specifically trying to convey, nor has he yet introjected the transitory identification that the patient is attempting to project. It is as though the therapist anticipates that some attempt to influence him is in the offing, either at the very outset or once the pressure is more actively underway, and he takes measures to prevent the process from going any further. The result is a sort of "undercooked" identification in which the interactional communication, whether verbal or nonverbal, is not allowed to develop.

A therapist may communicate this type of early short-circuiting of the empathic process by redirecting a patient's flow of associations, "setting limits" on a particular form of behavior, or challenging or denying a patient's perception of the therapist rather than remaining open to the potential impact such a fully developed communication might have. Consequently, the therapist conveys to the patient, with varying degrees of explicitness, that the therapist is experiencing discomfort and is not open to the continued reception of the particular communication which is being developed in the interaction.

As an example, a female patient who recently had experienced rejection by a man began her session by complaining about the high cost of treatment and its relative ineffectiveness in improving the quality of her life. When she began to question the continuation of her treatment, the therapist did not allow her to continue speaking of her sense of hopelessness with the treatment or her anger and contemplated rejection of him. On the contrary, he reacted to her complaints with thinly veiled annoyance, which was communicated both in his tone of voice and in his directing the patient away from these topics by asking her what she herself had actively done recently to pursue new relationships with men. Such a communication from the therapist directly conveyed to the patient that he was not willing to tolerate further interactional pressure aimed at communicating hopelessness, anger, and retaliatory impulses. In this instance, the therapist missed an opportunity to learn that the patient was unconsciously trying to communicate her own uncomfortable experience of feeling abandoned and unwanted by attempting to make the therapist feel the same way.

At the other extreme from the therapist who shuts off interactional pressure before the transient identification takes place is the therapist who disrupts the empathic process by adopting an "anything goes," laissez-faire posture. If the former class of disruption generates identifications that may be described as "undercooked," the latter scenario is associated with therapist identificatory experiences that are dramatically "overcooked." In extreme cases, the treatment situation comes to resemble a full-blown repetition of traumatic scenes from the patient's past. Disruptions of this variety are especially common among more disturbed patients. Freud (1914) first recognized that some patients could not recall events from the past but instead, tended to relive the experiences in the relationship with the therapist. Since that time, the element of reexperiencing the past in the therapeutic relationship has, of course, come to be viewed as an indispensable aspect of psychoanalytic treatment. Balint (1968, p. 146) referred to the phenomenon of reexperiencing as "therapeutic regression," distinguishing between "benign" versus "malignant" forms. The former produces positive recognition of core emotional concerns, leading to useful emotional discoveries and a "new beginning." In contrast, a "malignant regression" is thought to be motivated solely by a search for gratification by external action rather than emotional recognition; the demands for gratification from the therapist spiral in intensity, and a new beginning is never achieved.

It is possible for a therapist to gratify a patient not only through action, but also through inaction. Kernberg (1975) built upon Eissler's (1953) recommendation of the need for "parameters of techniques" with more disturbed patients. When, for example, a therapist allows a patient to scream at him for long periods of time, Kernberg argues, the patient is being provided with a destructive opportunity for gratification of aggressive instinctual drives. He suggests (pp. 185–190) various "modifications in technique" to provide necessary structure both outside the treatment and in the session itself (e.g., prohibition against destroying objects in the office). These modifications are essential for a predominantly interpretive treatment to occur.

It is sometimes difficult to distinguish the productive middle ground from the two extremes that constitute disruption at this subphase of the empathic process. From the perspective of countertransference, Flarsheim (1972) emphasizes that the therapist's personal tolerance level is an important consideration. Interactional pressure often takes place behaviorally around the ground rules and structural arrangements (cancellation policy, phone calls, timeliness of appointments and payment schedule) of the treatment. Unlike Langs (1982), who fervently asserted that there is one and only one way to "manage the frame," both Giovacchini (1972a) and Flarsheim proposed flexibility based on what the therapist can tolerate without coming to resent the patient.

Although the empathic process may not entirely fall apart until the next subphase or even later, in retrospect it can often be seen that the seeds of disruption were sown when the therapist, either by a laissez-faire passivity or by active collusion, permitted the patient's interactional pressure to exceed useful limits. Once a therapist begins to anticipate that one form or another of interactional pressure could very well go too far, how this is dealt with is critical because of the danger of error in the opposite extreme, "clamping down" too quickly. In the case of a new patient who begins to yell, the therapist must ask himself whether the increased volume seems to be serving any useful purpose and, second, whether he finds it disruptive to his own mental set. If there is no active verbal intervention from the therapist, does the patient settle down after having "ventilated" or does the patient escalate further?

In one such instance, a therapist developed a series of increasingly active interventions based on experience with a particular patient who was capable of screaming so loudly that not only was it impossible for therapist to attend, but sessions throughout the entire clinic were disrupted. The therapist would begin with simple observations calling attention to the rising volume. Often this was sufficient, but when it was not, the therapist would actively interject in an effort to inquire about and understand why the patient felt she needed to yell to get her message across. Every effort was made to try to approach the yelling in a calm, exploratory manner. If all such efforts failed to bring the patient's volume back to a more reasonable level, the therapist would ultimately remind the patient that the session needed to occur under circumstances that were tolerable for both parties. Since the patient knew from past experience that this was the therapist's position, they were then able to explore such possibilities as why the patient might be orchestrating a rejection by the therapist.

Of course, this series of interventions evolved with this patient over the course of many such experiences, and the empathic process involved elements that were much further along than the Interactional Pressure subphase. Nevertheless, the therapist's primary efforts were to address the patient's interactional pressure in order to render the experience manageable for both parties so that useful psychoanalytic work could occur. The alternative would have been either to clamp down too early and reject the patient before the projective identification could be transmitted, or simply to allow the abusive behavior to continue unchecked. For this particular patient, experience had demonstrated that the latter would have been tantamount to an untenable replay, with role reversal, of early experiences of child abuse, accompanied by the frightening sense that her therapist was as vulnerable to her onslaughts as she herself had been to her own mother's attacks. Premature limit-setting also would have been a reenactment of maternal abandonment, which constituted the other primary experience from the patient's early years. The therapist's task at the level of Interactional Pressure was to navigate a passage between these two danger situations.

SUBPHASE 3. IDENTIFICATION-SIGNAL AFFECT

Under optimal conditions in the empathic sequence, the therapist, having allowed the interactional pressure to unfold within workable limits, has an identificatory experience characterized by particular self-experiences and their associated affective states. The therapist can be thought of as having introjected a communication that exerts a modifying influence on his experience of self in the interaction. His affective reaction to the particular self-experience elicited by the immediate interaction optimally is a "signal affect" (Schafer, 1959; Zetzel,

1965; Olinick, 1969; Beres and Arlow, 1974). His tasks at this subphase level are to continue his receptivity, again within tolerable and reasonable limits, to the modification of his self-experience and to become aware of this shift in experience by recognizing the signal affects emanating from within that alert him to the possibility that an identification has been made. The nature and intensity of the interactional communication being processed vis-à-vis the therapist's capacity to tolerate the transitory modification of his self-experience largely determine the degree of awareness in the therapist of the identificatory experience.

Disruptions at this level are a consequence of a therapist's feeling either too uncomfortable or too gratified by the affective experience associated with the identification that has taken place. Defensive activity is then set in motion unconsciously by the therapist, blocking from consciousness the potential signal value of the affective impact of the identificatory experience. This defensive posture, for example, may surface in the therapist's becoming "too nice" in an attempt to compensate for unconscious guilt, anger, or sadistic impulses toward a patient. On the other hand, a therapist who feels gratified by a patient's idealization may block his pleasure from awareness by an excessively stiff or formal approach. For the therapist, the unfortunate outcome of his defensive activity is a countertransference impact without the absolutely vital awareness that this impact has occurred. Although a projective identification transmitted by the patient has taken hold within, the therapist cannot move forward in the Internal Processing phase without becoming more aware that this critical event has in fact taken place. The empathic process may simply arrest at this point. If the disruption is severe, a regression in the empathic process may also occur in which the therapist reacts to the unconscious identificatory experience by abruptly resisting, in one form or another, further interactional pressure without ever becoming aware of the underlying emotions that have been blocked from consciousness. A regression from this level may also disturb and disrupt a therapist's heretofore intact mental set.

The following clinical example illustrates how a disturbance at this level can be communicated to a patient. In the early stages of treatment, a female patient began calling her male therapist at home, complaining of being unable to tolerate her sense of loneliness and anxiety. The phone calls became regular events, with the patient describing some incident that day that had provoked her anxiety. She began each call with the statement, "I know you must hate me for calling you like this but I . . . ," a refrain she repeated throughout each call. She then would convey her immediate worry concerning some event and her doubt about the therapist's capacity to tolerate or help her. None of the so-called "crises" about which the patient called ever resulted in any self-destructive behavior on the patient's part. She remained punctual for her appointments and managed to perform her work responsibilities as usual.

The therapist initially responded to the calls with a sense of urgency and concern for the patient's immediate well-being, but he rapidly became uncomfortable with the constant intrusion into his home life and with his inability to help the patient modulate her frequent episodes of anxiety and neediness. The therapist was oblivious to the patient's projective identification, which had taken hold within him. He was conscious only of valiantly trying to help the patient and a global sense of discomfort at his failure to do so. Unaware of the affective signals (anger, exhaustion, and powerlessness) that accompanied the reception of the patient's projective identification, the therapist devised a plan for dealing with the patient that would "adequately address her needs." He recommended that she consult a psychiatrist for antianxiety medication. The patient followed the recommendation and received medication, only to terminate treatment shortly therafter.

Unable to tolerate a conscious awareness of himself as angry with the patient and exhausted and powerless in his efforts to help her, the therapist had blocked from consciousness the affective signals that he might otherwise have utilized to alert himself to the fact that he had received a projective identification. As a result, he could not apply his self-experience to increase his understanding of the patient and guide his interpretations. In contrast, his actions might well have been experienced by the patient as a recapitulation of the vicious circle of all her close relationships; namely, that the expression of neediness ultimately brings about the experience of rejection. The therapist's defensive denial of his affective reaction to the patient resulted in a failure to contain and ultimately to help the patient understand her own contribution to her problems in intimate relationships.

In summary, the Reception phase comprises three subphases: Reception, Interactional Pressure, and Identification-Signal Affect. In this opening phase of the empathic process, the therapist must first be able to clear his mind of outside preoccupations in order to attend adequately to the interactional presence of the patient; second, he must sustain a receptivity to verbal and nonverbal interactional pressure from the patient, within reasonable and tolerable limits, so that the patient has the opportunity to transmit projective identifications. Last, the therapist optimally recognizes his emotional response to the patient, not as a surface "reality," but as a signal affect, containing potentially valuable underlying meanings, which can alert the therapist to the fact that an identificatory experience has in fact occurred. A variety of disruptions can derail this opening phase. But once the therapist has in fact observed his emotional response to the patient as a signal affect, he is in a position to move forward into the phase of Internal Processing, the details of which are discussed in the next chapter.

6 *Internal Processing*

Having experienced an introjective identification in response to a projective identification from the patient, the therapist begins the work of the Internal Processing phase. Three distinct subphases are involved: the therapist attempts first to tolerate, then to examine, and ultimately to use his internal reaction as a tool for understanding the patient's experience. The work of the preceding Reception phase continues simultaneously in the background as the Internal Processing phase unfolds in the foreground.

SUBPHASE 4. CONTAINMENT-SEPARATENESS

At this subphase level, the task of the therapist is essentially twofold. First, the therapist is required to contain (Bion, 1959) and tolerate in consciousness his thoughts, feelings, and impulses having to do with himself, his patient, and their interaction. In contrast to the therapist whose progress has been halted at the Identification-Signal Affect subphase, the therapist at this level is aware of a change in his experiential state.

Consequently, the most basic disruption at this level results from the inability of the therapist to retain conscious awareness of the thoughts, feelings, and impulses associated with the introjective identification. A failure in containment is accompanied by defensive operations with which the therapist blocks from conscious awareness those aspects of his modified self-experience which he cannot tolerate.

For example, a therapist from whom a patient has elicited powerful feelings of hopelessness and inadequacy may suppress and deny these feelings because of his inability to tolerate such an experience of himself. This defensive posture is present in the therapist who responds to his patient's complaints that "the therapy just isn't helping" with a sort of all-knowing, "authoritative" attitude. The therapist may go so far as to state that the patient's difficulties at this juncture in treatment were predictable. In so doing, the therapist resists strong feelings of inadequacy induced by the patient's complaints and "failure to make progress." These feelings are unconsciously driven underground and replaced with an exaggerated, compensatory air of adequacy and expertise.

Alternatively, a failure at this most basic level of containment may result in a therapist's simply reacting to the experience, thereby discharging the associated impulses and relieving himself of the burden of containing his thoughts and feelings in consciousness. A therapist who feels ridiculed by a patient, for example, may react with some form of retaliation, ranging from a hostile interpretation to throwing the patient out of treatment under the guise of an "appropriate termination."

Building upon successful containment, the second task of this subphase requires that the therapist separate himself sufficiently from his own immediate experience to begin to observe and question the underlying sources of this experience in the interaction. To achieve a sense of separateness, the therapist must be able not only to contain his self-experience in consciousness, but also to establish sufficient "psychological distance" (Greenson, 1960) from the patient's interactional pressure and from the internal potency of the induced identification, with its related affects and impulses. In referring to the experience of psychological distance, we are not advocating mechanical remoteness on the therapist's part, a stance that is frequently justified in clinical circles as "maintaining technical neutrality." As Reik (1948) has pointed out, objectivity is not to be confused with inhumanness. What we are describing is an attempt by the therapist to be objective about his own *subjective* experience. By asking himself, What am I experiencing? the therapist lays the groundwork for the subsequent questions, Why am I feeling this way? How did this come about? What purposes might this serve for the patient to arouse this experience within me? Although these questions are more vigorously addressed in the next subphase, the effort to shift from a primarily subjective and experiential mode to one of predominant self-scrutiny may actually be accompanied by an immediate experience of greater comfort and spontaneity with the patient.

In addition to the therapist's conceptual framework and his current understanding of the therapeutic relationship, stability of personality, and cognitive-analytic ability, there appear to be three crucial elements in the establishment of the psychological distance inherent in the term separateness. First, the therapist must strive to suspend potential superego criticism (Fliess, 1942) and be able to experience himself in a temporarily unfavorable light. Second is the therapist's realization that the current self-experience, however uncomfortable, does not constitute an unmanageable threat to self-esteem when viewed in relation to a predominance of positive self-representations. Third, the therapist understands that the introjective identification is temporary. The therapist who establishes a sense of separateness acquires a perspective that reduces interactional and intrapsychic pressure and reaffirms the view that he is indeed the "author of his own feelings" (Ogden, 1979). Establishing separateness through these three crucial elements provides the necessary distance from the identificatory experience to further its examination. In the empathy literature, this is referred to as the shift from the experiencing ego to the observing ego. It is also at this point that the therapist's predominant mental set of "evenly hovering attention" shifts to a state of actively searching for meaning.

The failure to achieve sufficient separateness results in ongoing problems in retaining conscious awareness of the induced feeling state. At the opposite extreme, the therapist may remain all too aware of the induced feelings with no perspective on their underlying meaning. As an example of containment without separateness, a young therapist in training at a clinical facility for very disturbed chronic patients begins to experience himself as ineffectual and unable to help his patient "change." He quickly comes to the conclusion, based on his frustrating experience of himself, that he is not emotionally suited to treat patients with long-term emotional problems. Although he is able to hold this view of self in consciousness without blocking it from awareness or acting out the identification in the immediate treatment setting, he is unable to "pull back" sufficiently to begin to observe this experience as useful material that could help him understand his patient's experience of the world as unchanging and hopeless. The experience of self is taken literally, rather than as material to be observed. The sense of inadequacy is experienced as an enduring actuality rather than as a temporary and induced identification signaling something potentially important about the patient.

SUBPHASE 5. WORKING MODEL

The therapist's task in this subphase is to gather more detailed information about his own and the patient's immediate experience. Such empathic emotional information can be acquired only by steeping oneself in the experiential perspectives both of one self and of the patient. The therapist is able to gain a deeper understanding of these perspectives by focusing separately on the self- and object representation components of the "interactional introject", the structure that encompasses the internalized models of self and patient formed over time by the therapist.

The term working model was developed by Greenson (1960) to describe the therapist's "internal replica" of a patient built up and modified over time, consisting of the patient's "physical appearance, affects, life experiences, modes of behavior, attitudes, defenses, values, fantasies, etc." (p. 421). In the process of "listening through" the working model of the patient, the internal replica is shifted into the foreground of the listening process, while "all that is peculiarly or uniquely" the therapist is relegated to the background. Greenson developed the concept of the working model of the patient as a method for empathic listening because its active utilization produces affective associations to the patient's material that might not otherwise be accessible to therapist. We have proposed (Tansey and Burke, 1985) an expansion of Greenson's concept of the working model in two distinct ways. First, we have included in our conceptualization of working model an emphasis on the experience of the therapeutic interaction, both past and present. Thus, we speak of the patient-interaction working model rather than the patient working-model. Greenson's formulation predominantly addressed the experience of extratransference situations. Second, we have added a working model of the therapist, which we term the therapist-interaction working model. Greenson focused exclusively on a working model of the patient.

Our concept of the patient-interaction working model comprises all of Greenson's proposed patient characteristics, but also includes the therapist's observations of what seems to have been the patient's experience of the therapist (transference in its totalistic sense) and the therapeutic situation, both at any given moment and over the entire course of treatment. In agreement with Spence (1982) and Schafer (1980), we recognize that we are not referring to an internalized model of who the patient is, but rather an internalized replica of who the particular patient is for the particular therapist at any given moment. In utilizing this working model, the therapist attempts to relegate his own experience to the background, while devoting listening priority to his internal replica of the patient's experience of the immediate interaction.

Greenson (1960) introduced his construction of the working model by citing the following example:

> I had been treating a woman for several years and usually with good empathic understanding. In one hour she recounted the events of a weekend and focused in particular on a Saturday night party. Suddenly she began to cry. I was puzzled. I was not "with it"—the crying left me cold—I couldn't understand it. I realized that I had been partially distracted by something she had said. At the party she mentioned a certain analyst and I had become sidetracked, wondering why he was present. Quickly reviewing the events she had recounted, I found no

> clues. I then shifted from listening from the 'outside' to participant listening. I went to the party as if I were the patient. Now something clicked—an "aha" experience. A fleeting event told to me as the outsider had eluded me; now in my empathy this event illuminated the crying. At the party a woman had graciously served the patient with a copious portion of food. To me as the observer, this event was meaningless. But to me as the experiencer, this woman instantly stirred up the picture of the patient's good-hearted and big-breasted nursemaid. The "aha" I experienced was my sudden recognition of this previously anonymous figure. Now I shifted back to the position of observer and analyzer. Yes the longing for the old nursemaid had come up in the last hour. In the meantime the patient herself had begun to talk of the nursemaid. My empathic discovery seemed to be valid. When the analyst's association precedes and coincides with the patient's, it confirms that the analyst is on the right track [p. 421].

Greenson makes a crucial distinction between the type of trial identification that is commonly confused with empathy and the empathic trial identification of the patient-interaction working model. He states that he went to the party "as if I were the patient." This listening perspective is to be distinguished from "as if I were in the patient's situation." By "listening through the working model," Greenson is not listening as if he were himself in the patient's situation, but rather as if he were the patient in the patient's situation. While the former mode of listening can be used as a source of comparison, it does not provide the potentially intimate correspondence with the patient's subjective experience offered by listening through the patient-interaction working model. Greenson's clinical example clearly illustrates that the task of the therapist in the patient-interaction working model is to assume what he considers to be the subjective perspective of the patient.

The therapist's internal replica of his *own* experience of the interaction—the therapist-interaction working model—consists of all of the characteristics that Greenson suggests, only now with reference to the therapist rather than to the patient. In addition, it includes the therapist's internal replica of himself as he has experienced working with a particular patient in a particular therapeutic relationship, both at any given moment as well as over the entire course of treatment. We prefer the term therapist-interaction working model to the less cumbersome term therapist working model, because it emphasizes our view that the subjective experience of the therapist cannot be understood in isolation from the unique characteristics of the particular interaction with each patient. In so doing, we build upon Winnicott's (1960) observation that "there is no such thing as an infant" (p. 39), by which he meant that an infant cannot be understood in isolation from the mother-infant unity. Similarly, the subjective experiences of both patient and therapist are best understood in the context of the interaction from which they arise.

Within the therapist-interaction working model with any given patient, various self-qualifies tend to predominate that differ from those which are highlighted with other patients. Although there may be a certain core experience of self, along the lines of the characteristics that Greenson proposes, which forms the basis of the therapist-interaction working model, there are additional characteristics superimposed upon this core experience which pertains to our unique experiences with each patient. For example, with a particular patient at a particular time, a therapist may view himself as competent, warm, humorous, and helpful. Yet his work with the next patient he sees may leave him with transient feelings of boredom, depression, and inadequacy. Just as each therapist internalizes a different therapist-interaction working model with each patient, this internalized replica shifts and fluctuates to some extent with a given patient at different points in time.

When the therapist "listens through" the therapist-interaction working model, he shifts the focus on the patient's experience to the background while bringing his own experience of the interaction into the foreground. Although the therapist continues to listen to and receive communications from the patient, he devotes primary attention to the fullest possible awareness of his own thoughts, feelings, and impulses while simultaneously attempting to recognize what is occurring in the interaction that might give rise to this experience of himself.

The patient-interaction and the therapist-interaction working models allow the therapist to deepen his understanding of both himself and the patient. Through an exploration of both models, the therapist can take more active control over a process that heretofore he has experienced only as a passive recipient. Together, the therapist-interaction and the patient-interaction working models make up the therapist's "interactional introject." During the Working Model subphase, the therapist selects which component of the interactional introject he needs to call into the foreground of his listening perspective in order to navigate this important juncture in the empathic process.

Rather than being a prescribed sequence in which the therapist must utilize the two working models, there is virtually always a shifting back and forth between models when this process goes well. The achievements of this subphase lay the groundwork for the insights that are subsequently established in the Empathic Connection subphase. At this advanced stage in the processing of an introjective identification, however, a therapist will often oscillate rapidly and freely between the Working Model and Empathic Connection subphases, so much so that an argument could be made for eliminating the term subphases in favor of the term aspects in order to prevent temporal confusion. The term subphases will suffice only if we keep in mind that this process involves a fluid and dynamic interplay of events as opposed to a rigid sequence.

There are two distinct levels of disruption in the empathic process within the Working Model subphase. At the most basic level, the therapist is unable to accomplish the analytic tasks inherent in either working model. Although he may be able to observe himself or his patient in a global way on the basis of the achievements of the previous subphase, the failure to listen through each of the internal replicas leaves the therapist's emotional and cognitive knowledge fragmented, amorphous, and incomplete. In such an instance the therapist would have contained the identificatory experience but be unable to gather the emotional knowledge necessary to make sense out of his and the patient's experience. This level of disruption may be due to the disturbing feelings within the therapist associated with an increase in awareness of his own or the patient's current experiential state.

The second level of disruption is represented by a successful utilization of only one or the other of the two working models. More commonly, the therapist will have an easier time with the patient-interaction working model than with the therapist-interaction working model, since the latter involves looking inward to examine what are often painful, objectionable, unpleasant, or even exciting experiences of self. Knowledge of only one model severely limits the empathic process by restricting the informational base for interventions.

To illustrate, a therapist finds himself feeling a mounting sense of annoyance with a patient who frequently requests appointment changes, manifestly as a consequence of demands of business travel. Although the therapist is aware of his annoyance, he does not understand with any depth the specific sources and meanings of this reaction. Analytic work can break down at this point if the therapist merely dismisses his irritation and offers alternative times or, conversely, reacts in an angry, withholding, rigid, or punitive fashion under the banner of "preserving the frame." The opportunity would be lost to examine further what the patient might unconsciously be trying to communicate to the therapist by eliciting annoyance in this way. On the other hand, if the therapist uses his feeling of annoyance as a signal that something meaningful is happening that requires elucidation, he can then examine himself through the therapist-interaction working model. He may discover that his feeling of annoyance is a manifestation of deeper feelings of being manipulated, controlled by the patient, and pushed to react in either a punitive or a self-depreciating manner. The empathic work of this subphase would remain incomplete if the therapist did not then shift his attention to the patient-interaction working model, through which the patient's possible sense of entitlement in conjunction with fears of rejection might be better understood.

SUBPHASE 6. EMPATHIC CONNECTION

Once the therapist has fulfilled the tasks of the Working Model subphase, he is in a position to explore if, how, and why his own experiential state and that of the patient may relate to one another. The working models described in the prior subphase are continually reemployed by the therapist to explore each of these questions. It is here, in the Empathic Connection subphase, that the therapist has the opportunity to examine through the working models the extent to which his own experience of the interaction is indeed projectively determined.

In order to facilitate the presentation of the schema, we shall only touch upon the question of validation at this juncture; our more extensive examination of this critical clinical issue is found in chapter 8.

The first task facing the therapist is to determine whether in fact there is a connection or correspondence between his own and the patient's emotional state. As mentioned earlier, there are three categories of interactional fit between the therapist's and the patient's experience characterized by the types of introjective identification aroused within the therapist that are outlined by Racker (1957). The first category involves a concordant identification in the therapist in which the immediate self-experiences of both participants are similar in some significant way. A patient sobbing over the death of a beloved pet, which elicits from the therapist feelings of grief and a suppressed impulse to cry, is a clear illustration of a concordant interactional fit, though the experiences of each participant differ in the degree of intensity. Concordant identifications are traditionally associated with empathy and not with projective identification. We are proposing that concordant identifications are indeed a reflection of the therapist's reception of the patient's projective identification.

The second category of interactional fit results from the patient's influencing the therapist to identify with an internalized object representation of the patient's (as opposed to a self-representation, as in the concordant linkage) eventuating in a complementary (Deutsch, 1926; Racker, 1957) identification in the therapist. The often stormy consequences of complementary role enactments, in contrast to the concordant category, are usually associated with projective identification, though not with the potentially empathic outcome we are attempting to elucidate. The patient, for example, who experiences life and relationships as barren and ungiving may well elicit, through interactional pressure, an impulse within the therapist to deprive or withhold from the patient in some way.

The third category of interactional fit involves elements that are both concordant and complementary in nature, as illustrated by the masochistic patient who transiently assumes the sadistic role in the therapeutic interaction. The therapist's temporary masochistic identification awakened by the pressure of the interaction is both complementary with the patient's immediate sadistic self-representation, and concordant with the patient's prevailing, longstanding experience of self-as-victim.

The therapist determines whether or not there is a connection between his own and the patient's experience by listening once again to the interaction through both working models. This reemployment of the working models allows the therapist to immerse himself in the emotional experience of himself and the patient in an attempt to test his hypothesis as to the concordant or complementary correspondence between these experiential states. The therapist uses the working models to review what has transpired, including the patient's material, the interactional cues, the manner in which his own feelings began to surface, the adaptive context for the current material, and the like. From this reexperiencing of the session, the therapist can search for potential links between his own and the patient's experience. Having ascertained a correspondence does not in and of itself mean that projective identification from the patient is involved in any significant way. For example, the existence of a complementary correspondence between a therapist's feeling uncharacteristically annoyed and a patient's feeling "picked on" may have more to do with the therapist's having a bad day than with interactional pressure from the patient evoking a hostile response. Again, we refer the reader to chapter 8 for a detailed exegesis of the validating process.

The second task of this subphase is to determine the conscious or unconscious communicative meanings underlying the patient's attempt to construct a particular concordant or complementary arrangement of experiential roles for himself and the therapist. There appear to be two such categories of meaning. First, there is the question of the unconscious message that is being communicated to the therapist through the patient's projective identification. This dynamic meaning may be broad or narrow in scope. Its essential element may relate to distant genetic history that is being reenacted, or it may primarily be an attempt to communicate something much more immediate, as in the case of the patient who elicits feelings of worthlessness in his therapist soon after the announcement of a vacation by the therapist. Such a scenario may well represent an interactional attempt to turn the tables in order to communicate to the therapist how it feels to be left behind. Second, in addition to what is being communicated through the patient's projective identification, there is a level of meaning concerning how the patient feels communicating this specific message to the therapist. A patient who consciously or unconsciously causes a therapist to feel victimized may then experience intense fears of retaliation, again at a conscious or unconscious level. Both types of meaning may be ascertained only by the therapist's utilization of the two working models to reassess the emotional experience of himself and the patient and to gather more information to substantiate potential meanings underlying the patient's interactional communications. The subject of underlying meaning as an important validation criterion is explored in chapter 8.

Corresponding to each of the two tasks of this subphase are distinct levels of empathic disruption. The therapist may be unable to assess the correspondence (concordant, complementary, or both) between his own and the patient's experience. He may fail to understand the concrete interactional elements that gave rise to his own and the patient's subjective experience. For example, a therapist may recognize a feeling of annoyance with his patient whom he perceives as increasingly helpless and dependent without being able to see how these experiential roles are dynamic counterparts. Although there is room for disruption at this level, the assessment of the actual correspondence or role configuration should be relatively straightforward if the therapist has indeed successfully utilized both working models in the previous subphase.

Similarly, the therapist may fail to understand adequately the two types of meaning for the patient that underlie a particular projective identification. As we have described elsewhere (Tansey and Burke, 1985), we concur with Ogden (1979, 1982) and Grotstein (1981) that it is useful to view the patient's projective identification as an effort to communicate to the therapist in a way that is potentially much more effective and powerful than words alone. The therapist who is unable to fathom the meanings beneath the construction of a particular role relationship is missing critical elements of empathic emotional knowledge and is impeded in achieving optimal empathic contact with his patient. In the example cited earlier, the therapist might be aware that his annoyance is related in a complementary manner to the patient's current state of helpless, dependent longing, but he may not understand why the patient would unconsciously construct such a configuration of experiential roles or how it makes the patient feel to engage in this particular form of communication with the therapist at this particular time.

Having examined the pathways and pitfalls by which a therapist internally processes the patient's impact upon him, we shall turn our attention in the next chapter to the process of "giving back" to the patient.

7 *The Communication Phase*

Empathy is often described as an intrapsychic rather than an interpersonal phenomenon. Not only does it seem to be conceptualized as though the patient has nothing to do with the therapist's singlehanded acquisition of empathic insight, empathy is sometimes viewed as ending with what the therapist understands internally. In contrast, we would propose that the empathic process not only involves taking in the patient's influence (Reception), followed by analyzing and arriving at tentative understandings of this material (Internal Processing), but also entails the process of "giving back" to the patient. Questions of what, when, and how a therapist communicates to a patient, both with respect to verbal (especially interpretive) and nonverbal channels, are not merely matters of technique and timing. Answering these technical questions requires an immediate and in-depth empathic sensitivity to the patient and to the status of the interaction.

We have outlined a Communication phase of the empathic process that encompasses the therapist's assessment and actual implementation of giving something back to the patient from the emotional knowledge he has gathered, with regard to both the timing and the content of an intervention. The ultimate goal of this exchange is the promotion of the patient's insight into his own psychological makeup. This, in turn, paves the way for a new interpersonal experience with the therapist, one in which the potentially destructive impact of the patient's projective identification is contained and utilized by the therapist to illuminate highly significant aspects of the patient's internal and interpersonal worlds. Through empathic awareness, for example, the re-creation in the therapeutic interaction of a patient's repetitively destructive sadomasochistic paradigm in close relationship can be contained and constructively examined rather than blindly played out. This new experience for the patient, in contrast to his longstanding belief that the world consists only of those who attack and those who are victims, provides a new model of what can happen in human relationships, reminiscent of what Balint (1968) referred to as a new beginning. The patient then has the opportunity to internalize this new object relationship, consolidated through insight, as a model and a foundation for seeking more satisfying relationships in life.

In this third phase of the empathic process, the therapist conveys through verbal and nonverbal channels, in both implicit and explicit ways, the extent to which the projective identification from the patient has been processed through the Reception and the Internal Processing phases. It goes without saying that some form of communication with each patient is ongoing from the very first moment of initial contact, usually over the telephone. Communication specifically pertaining to what would be considered a patient's "successful" projective identification (that is, one that hits home in the therapist) is actually begun in the Reception phase, prior to extensive internal processing, from the moment that the therapist becomes aware of a signal affect heralding that an identification within the therapist has in fact been induced. At every phase and subphase level, there is some degree of interactional communication from the therapist to the patient, whether verbal or nonverbal, concerning either the readiness to receive the patient's projective identification (Mental Set and Interactional Pressure subphases) or the actual status of that reception once it has occurred (Identification-Signal Affect subphase, all three subphases of Internal Processing).

The three communication subphases are arranged according to the degree of empathic understanding that the therapist makes *explicit* to the patient. As indicated in the discussions of the Working Model and Empathic Connection subphases, there are three areas pertaining to the processing of a particular projective identification upon which any interpretive intervention from the therapist may build: the therapist's understanding of the patient's experience, the therapist's understanding of his own experience, and the possible connections between the two. The subphases progress from those interventions involving no explicit interpretation of any of the three areas to interventions that explicitly attempt to illuminate either the patient's or the therapist's experience, and, finally, to interpretations that explicitly posit a relationship between both participants' experiences.

Because the therapist needs to weigh the critical factors of timing and technique, the degree of explicitness may or may not parallel the complexity and depth of his understanding of the relationship between his own and the patient's experience. Therefore, the therapist may very well arrive at a highly sophisticated hypothesis regarding the connection between his own experience and the patient's, and yet, for reasons of timing and sensitivity to what are seen to be the patient's needs at a particular moment, the therapist may elect to make no explicit verbal communication to the patient.

The depth and breadth of the therapist's understanding of his own experience, his patient's experience, and the vicissitudes of the interaction will determine what he is *able* to say; timing considerations guide the decisions as to what is *advisable* to say. Earlier we made the point that in the development of this schema, the notion of "aspects" of processing held some advantage over "subphases" because of the potential for temporal confusion and sequential inflexibility in the latter term. Similarly, we realize that the term "options" in some ways is better suited to our communication "subphases," since in a given clinical situation, saying nothing may be a more useful communication than an interpretation. Even though an interpretation in our schema is depicted as a more advanced subphase of communication, it is not necessarily a better option than silent formulating, depending on the therapist's assessment of how useful or disruptive a particular interpretation may be to a given patient at a given time. The clinical illustrations provided are intended to clarify this point. For reasons of consistency, we are retaining subphases in our terminology.

Some schools of psychoanalytic thought emphasize extratransference or genetic material, whereas others focus predominantly on the immediate therapeutic interaction as a mutually determined process. Although our own orientation favors an examination of the patient-therapist relationship, our communication schema may be applied equally well to those emphasizing genetic or extratransference interventions.

A final introductory comment to the Communication subphases: Considerable potential for misunderstanding arises in connection with certain interpretive communications that entail elements of countertransference disclosure. Direct mention of the therapist's experience to a patient is a very delicate matter deserving much consideration before its introduction into the therapeutic interaction. How such a reference to the therapist's experience is presented depends on clinical orientation and technique. In any case, we are not recommending that a therapist simply unload his personal thoughts and feelings onto the patient. But neither do we advocate a phobic attitude (Little, 1951) toward countertransference disclosure. Any countertransference disclosure is usefully employed only in the context of the therapist's attempt to discover how his understanding of his own experience enhances his understanding of the patient's experience. In the overwhelming majority of instances, the therapist is better advised not to disclose direct countertransference material, but rather to make silent use of his responses to the patient in an effort to guide interpretations pertaining primarily to the patient's subjective experience. For a more comprehensive discussion of this point, see chapter 9, which elucidates the uses and abuses of countertransference disclosure.

SUBPHASE 7. NONINTERPRETIVE COMMUNICATION

In this subphase, the therapist does not engage in verbal communication that explicitly focuses on the patient's projective identification, though verbal exchanges dealing with other material may take place. The absence of such interventions may be attributable to one of two reasons. First, the therapist may have not yet arrived at an adequate empathic understanding of the nature of the projective identification, either because the identification has not yet been fully received or because the therapist is still in an early stage of internal processing. Second, as noted previously, the therapist may have a very sophisticated understanding of the connection between his own and the patient's experience but choose to remain silent for reasons of timing and technique.

Especially in the latter instance, the therapist nonverbally conveys a great deal to the patient about the impact of the projective identification. This is communicated through the standard channels of nonverbal communication, such as facial expression and tone of voice, as well as by other observable actions on the therapist's part to which the patient may be quite vigilant. Examples of such actions that convey disruption include drifting attention, sullen withdrawal, lateness for appointments, extreme flexibility or inflexibility regarding the rescheduling of appointments or the timeliness of payment, and the like. Similarly, consistency, reliability, and the absence of signs of empathic disruption may be very reassuring to a patient who is fearful of the potentially destructive impact of a projective identification.

Langs (1975, 1976, 1978) has written a number of volumes on how the therapist communicates disturbance at this level through the failure of strict "maintenance of the therapeutic frame." Although Langs's position has merit, in his vehement emphasis on what he believes to be *the single and universal way* to manage the groundrules of treatment, he ignores the individual differences of patients and therapists. The rigidity of his position in attacking all forms of groundrule flexibility is itself suggestive of empathic disruption, albeit at the other extreme from the therapist who is too accommodating. Either polarity may well represent a noninterpretive communication to the patient that the therapist is having difficulty with a projective identification.

The optimal course of noninterpretive communication is not a charade of "acceptance," especially when the therapist is feeling a great deal of pressure to discharge impulses associated with the induced identification. Rather, the therapist may be in the experiential position of needing to hold his tongue until he is able to gain the necessary perspective from which to make use of what he is experiencing. The therapist's efforts to countervail feelings of hurt, anger, or depression with expressions of "unconditional positive regard" can only be viewed as defensive in nature. It is sometimes only with great effort that the therapist is able to maintain, if not neutrality, at least equanimity in the face of interactional pressure.

SUBPHASE 8. TRANSFERENCE-BASED OR COUNTERTRANSFERENCE-BASED COMMUNICATION

This subphase pertains to communications from the therapist that *explicitly* refer to his understanding of either his own experience or that of the patient. The former is referred to as a countertransference-based communication, the latter a transference-based communication. Once again, it is the material that is made *explicit* to the patient which distinguishes the two types of communications. This subphase parallels the Working Model subphase, and the formulation that is made explicit to the patient is grounded in the emotional knowledge derived from this prior subphase.

In a transference-based communication, the therapist makes explicit references to the patient's experience, drawing primarily on emotional knowledge acquired from the patient-interaction working model. The utilization of transference-based communications may arise from several different circumstances. The therapist may employ this type of communication even though he has not advanced very far in the therapist-interaction working model and has little depth of understanding of his own subjective experience. Similarly, the therapist may have no clear sense of the nature of a potential connection, whether complementary or concordant, between his own experience and that of the patient. By contrast, the therapist may in fact have a complex understanding of both his own experience with the patient and of the nature of the interactional connection, but for reasons of timing and technique may limit himself to an intervention that *explicitly* refers only to the patient's experience.

To illustrate a transference-based communication, we take the case of a patient who is extremely apprehensive about the serious illness and impending surgery of his child. In the sessions immediately preceding the surgery, the patient engages in frequent sarcasm aimed at the therapist's competence and the value of the treatment. The patient at one point comments, "I've had about enough of you and your psychological platitudes. The only one who is getting anything out of this treatment is you because of your ridiculously high fee. I would have done better to spend the money on vacations than to have allowed myself to be conned into coming here."

The therapist is initially stung by the patient's comments but is then able to pull back from the signal affects of hurt and a wish to retaliate. By adopting the listening perspective of the patient-interaction working model and imagining himself to be this patient talking to this therapist, in this way, at this particular time, the therapist is able to "taste" (Fliess, 1942) his patient's anger. But the therapist-as-patient is aware that he is also very fearful for his son's safety and well-being, although this fear has been forced into the background of experience by the more comfortable, familiar, and safer feelings of anger. The therapist then imagines himself as the patient responding at this moment to an intervention aimed at illuminating the defensive use of anger, and he envisions himself suddenly feeling openly sad and afraid. Without engaging in any further examination of his own (that is, the therapist-as-therapist) subjective experience by means of the listening perspective of the therapist-interaction working model, the therapist offers, "Despite the fact that to all appearances you seem so angry, I can't help but feel that somehow it is more comfortable for you to be angry with me right now than to be left with just how afraid you are about your son."

In a countertransference-based interpretation, the therapist makes *explicit* reference to the emotional knowledge he has derived from the therapist-interaction working model. Again, he may have little sense of either the patient's experience or the connection between his own and the patient's experience. Alternatively, the therapist may have a well-examined hypothesis about what the patient is experiencing as well as the interactional connection, but for reasons of timing and technique, he may refer explicitly only to an interpretation that builds on his own countertransference response. It bears repeating here that this is an area with substantial room for the empathic process to derail in the form of ill-advised countertransference disclosure (see chapter 9).

To illustrate a countertransference-based communication, we might take the same scenario involving the man who feels very afraid in anticipation of his son's surgery. This time, in response to the patient's sarcasm and devaluation, the therapist observes in himself the signal affects of narcissistic injury and an impulse to retaliate. After successfully pulling back from the identificatory experience, the therapist might just as well have begun with the therapist-interaction listening perspective rather than that of the patient-interaction working model as in the previous example.

From the listening perspective of the therapist-interaction working model, the therapist experiences himself as acutely concerned for his patient regarding the son's illness. But at the same time, he is aware that this concern is being forced into the background by the feelings of defensiveness and annoyance elicited by the patient's attack. With this emotional knowledge in mind, but without making immediate use of the listening perspective of the patient-interaction working model, the therapist might intervene with a countertransference-based communication: "I feel as though I am being pulled into a fight here at a time when your son's illness seems so pressing. Do you suppose there is anything to that?" By intervening in this fashion, the therapist is building upon what he hypothesizes to be an induced response to the patient, elicited via the patient's projective identification. The therapist does this with the clear intention of attempting to understand better what is taking place with his patient by first understanding what is happening within himself and then building an interpretation based on this understanding.

SUBPHASE 9. TRANSFERENCE/COUNTERTRANSFERENCE-BASED COMMUNICATIONS

At this final subphase of the empathic process, the therapist engages in communications to the patient that explicitly refer to the experience of both participants. This type of communication builds upon insight and information acquired through the listening perspectives of both working models. In addition, transference/countertransference-based communications evolve from the integrative understanding derived from the Empathic Connection subphase of Internal Processing, in which the therapist comes to understand the concordant or complementary correspondence between what the patient and the therapist are experiencing. Even at this advanced level of intervention, the depth and degree of sophistication of the therapist's communication will vary. Once again, the variability may be attributable either to the level of the therapist's understanding or to considerations of timing and technique. The therapist, for example, may limit himself to an intervention that merely refers to the subjective experience of both participants in the interaction, delineating what seems to be either the concordant or complementary nature of the connection between the two. In an effort to illuminate the connection between what each is experiencing without becoming more ambitious in exploring potential underlying meanings of this role relationship, the therapist from the foregoing example might comment, "I feel as though you may be trying to put distance between us by starting a fight."

Having established this complementary correspondence in his own mind, the therapist might then try to dig deeper into why the patient might be trying to create distance. At this juncture, the therapist once again utilizes the listening perspectives of the therapist-interaction and patient-interaction working models. Within the former listening perspective, the therapist places his own immediate experience of the interaction into the foreground. As in the earlier illustration, he becomes aware of true concern for his patient regarding the son's illness but realizes that this concern has been partially pushed into the background by the feelings of defensiveness and annoyance elicited by the patient's attack. The therapist then shifts to the listening perspective of the patient-interaction working model.

As in the earlier example of a transference-based intervention, the therapist, by imagining himself to be the patient, is able to feel what he believes to be the quality of his patient's anger. He also senses that this anger feels more comfortable and less threatening than his fear for his son's well-being, which has been pushed into the background of consciousness by his angry tirade. The emotional knowledge he has thus acquired enables the therapist to see the fit very clearly between his own concern (overshadowed by defensiveness and irritation) and the patient's fear (obfuscated by an angry tirade). With this understanding, the therapist then formulates the following interpretation. Once again, before presenting it to the patient, he returns to the patient-interaction working model and imagines the patient's possible response before intervening: "I think you are very afraid about what is happening with your son. But in an effort to keep both of us away from how overwhelmed you feel about that, I believe you may be trying to pick a fight so as to keep me at arm's length."

In this intervention, the therapist attempts to illuminate the patient's underlying experience of being overwhelmed with fear and concern for his son, as well as the manner in which he is struggling to cope with this experience, both from an intrapsychic and interpersonal point of view. The therapist uses all three sources of emotional knowledge about the patient—his understanding of his own experience, the patient's experience, and the interactional connection between the two—in an effort to "give back" this understanding to the patient. By observing the patient's response to his intervention, the therapist has the opportunity to make judgments about the accuracy of his interpretive hypotheses.

A more ambitious communication at this level would attempt to penetrate into deeper unconscious meanings underlying the patient's interactional communications. To illustrate with the same clinical situation, if the patient is responsive to the intervention just mentioned, the therapist might move ahead with interpretations that draw upon additional insight gained from the listening perspectives we have outlined. Returning to the therapist-interaction working model, the therapist pays closer attention to the feeling of defensiveness and irritation elicited in him by the patient's verbal assault. He recalls that had he given full rein to his impulses as the patient was attacking, rather than attending to these impulses as signals, he might well have said to the patient, "If that's how you feel, get the hell out." Especially given his awareness of his concern for the patient at this time of crisis, the therapist feels convinced that the strength of his response to the patient's tirade somehow has still deeper meaning than the formulation already established.

He then brings the listening perspective of the patient-interaction working model to the foreground to explore this area further. By imagining himself to be the patient being thrown out of his therapist's office, he becomes vividly aware of a flood of memories from his childhood. On many occasions the patient had spoken of his parents' unrealiability as sources of support to whom he might turn when he felt afraid, sad, anxious, or lonely. At such times, there were loud arguments about trivial matters and he was sent off to his room. Seeing the connections between his own impulses to reject the patient and the patient's own early experiences in childhood and adolescence, the therapist, after imagining how the patient might respond, offered the following transference-countertransference-based interpretation:

> The question arises as to what it means that you would want to keep us both away from how afraid you are feeling inside behind the wall of anger you've been trying to erect. I think it is possible that if you were to let me know just how vulnerable and afraid you are feeling about your son, and how much you need my support, you feel convinced that I won't come through for you, that I will be repulsed by your needing something from me.

From this point, it could be possible to incorporate an understanding of the patient's genetic experiences that resemble the current scenario and are being relived. It could also be possible to clarify the manner in which the patient's actions tend to bring on the very outcome that is so painful, thus repeating the vicious circle and reconfirming the self-fulfilling prophecy that others cannot be trusted in times of need. This exploration would be possible only if the interpretation continued to be supported by the patient's reaction, and the genetic focus did not seem to be a further form of flight from the intensity of the immediate feelings in the therapeutic interaction.

8 *Validation*

The totalist perspective toward countertransference firmly established within psychoanalytic theory the notion that a therapist's emotional responses to a patient—even those of a powerful and unpleasant nature—may provide a pathway to empathic understanding that would otherwise be inaccessible. At the same time, led by Annie Reich (1951), the classical view of countertransference warned against the reckless conclusion that a therapist's emotional response to a patient was necessarily induced by the patient. This extremely useful caveat pointed to the need for a validating methodology. Despite the passage of nearly 40 years since Reich's paper, strikingly little has been done to develop this methodology. Edelson (1984) argued passionately for psychoanalysis to respond to mounting criticism that its reasoning and process of investigation were unscientific by constructing appropriate measures and methodology by which hypotheses could be tested. From a purely theoretical perspective, Langs (1976) and Ogden (1982) have made beginning efforts in the area of validation of countertransference. From a quantitative perspective, several researchers (Cutler, 1958; Kernberg et al., 1972; Mintz, Luborsky, and

Auerback, 1971; Singer and Luborsky, 1978) have focused either on demonstrating the existence of countertransference reactions or on the impact of these reactions on the psychotherapeutic process. We know of no attempts to develop a procedure for validating hypotheses concerning the potential usefulness of specific countertransference responses as they occur in the clinical setting.

Given that the need for such a procedure is so glaringly apparent, the question immediately arises why more attention has not been paid to this area. We attribute this absence to two factors. First, developing a methodology for validating clinical hypotheses is an extremely difficult and elusive task regardless of the material that is involved. The areas of dream analysis, transference analysis, genetic reconstruction, and the interpretation of projective testing (despite its more objective and scientific aura) all demonstrate the complexity of applying a validating process to clinical phenomena. Second, of all the varieties of source material from which clinical hypotheses are constructed, countertransference material is by far the most difficult to work with reliably. This is true because the therapist is at the experiential center of that which he is attempting to examine with a necessary degree of "objectivity." Thus, he is required to objectify his own subjectivity, a task that is fraught with many more and deeper pitfalls than other sources of clinical inference.

It must be admitted at the outset that any attempt to establish irrefutable proof that a countertransference response has this or that meaning is doomed to failure. We are referring here to complex human interaction, the meanings of which are often multiple and contradictory, characterized by ambivalence, conflict, and the tension between latent and manifest communication. Inferrence is at the heart of any attempt to interpret meaning, and inference itself necessarily presumes judgment and opinion. Though not specifically with reference to countertransference material, Spence (1982) argued that the formulation of an interpretation tends to create truth rather than discover it. But despite these epistemological problems, we can nevertheless aspire to become more systematic in our efforts to formulate and validate our hypotheses. In this regard, Schafer (1954, pp. 142–148) referred to the need for converging lines of inference from a variety of sources in the formulation and validation of Rorschach interpretations. The same principle of convergence applies to the formulation and validation of clinical hypotheses built upon countertransference material.

Validation of clinical hypotheses of any sort refers not to an absolute and final event, but rather to an ongoing and progressive refinement of understanding. In keeping with the principle of convergence, we believe that our schema for the processing of interactional communications offers a framework within which to seek progressively higher degrees of confidence in the validity of hypotheses pertaining to countertransference material. The potential danger in using unvalidated countertransference reactions in the interaction with the patient is obvious. Our discussion in chapter 9 on the uses and abuses of countertransference disclosure spells out many of the instances in which the therapist's lack of thoughtful validation can have a negative impact on the therapeutic relationship.

Probably the single most frequent example of employing countertransference reactions without substantial validation is the therapist who experiences a strong emotional reaction in direct relation to a patient's interactional presence and then assumes that the reaction was "induced" by the patient and represents a direct, point-for-point correspondence with what the patient was unconsciously attempting to communicate. Rather than treating his emotional reaction as a hypothetical cue that may lead toward a better understanding of the patient, the therapist makes an unexamined assumption that the patient has put that particular emotional state "into" him. The evidence that might substantiate or refute such a conclusion remains unexplored. We believe that the criteria presented in this chapter can aid a therapist who is motivated to examine both the degree of influence from the patient and the contribution the therapist himself makes by way of his own personal tendencies.

If we are to view our countertransference reactions as important sources of emotional information about the patient and the treatment process, then we must be able to trust that the relevance of these countertransference reactions can be determined through criteria that provide a series of reliable checks and balances. With the ability to make systematic assessments about the extent of our own personal contribution comes a stronger inclination to seek an active emotional sensitivity to the patient's communications and less inhibition to examine our emotional responsiveness.

Countertransference-based hypothesis formulation and the concomitant need for validation is set in motion from the point at which a therapist becomes aware of a signal affect heralding the possibility that a transient identification has taken place. There are two overlapping areas that require elucidation. First, what is the *source* of the particular emotional response to the patient? To what extent is this response subtly or grossly induced by the patient? Conversely, to what extent does this response reflect the therapist's own emotional propensities having little or nothing to do with the patient? Second, if it is determined that the countertransference response is largely induced by the patient's projective identification, what is the *meaning* of this event for the patient? Both areas of exploration —source and meaning—require a process of hypothesis formulation followed by an effort to establish a sufficient degree of confidence in the validity of the given formulation. The therapist must seek converging lines of inference in attempting to confirm his construal of both the source and the meanings of any given countertransference response.

SOURCE HYPOTHESES

Let us turn first to the question of source. The therapist may have an immediate hunch about the genesis of his response. This would be true, for example, in the case of the therapist who is feeling uncharacteristically dispirited while being attacked by a patient for not being more helpful. The therapist's immediate hypothesis would likely be that the patient had induced feelings of inadequacy within him. This source hypothesis would then await further investigation along the lines we will be suggesting. Conversely, the therapist may immediately suspect that his response emanates predominantly from self-generated concerns rather than from an identificatory experience induced by the patient. Such might be the case when the therapist finds that she has a very hard time keeping her attention from drifting, while at the same time she realizes that she did not sleep well the previous night and, furthermore, that she was not able to focus her attention as well as usual with patients earlier the same day.

In the absence of an immediate hunch as to the source of his emotional experience with the patient, the therapist must pursue an open-ended inquiry. In so doing, it is essential that he examine both his own propensities and the role the patient may be pressuring him to occupy; as Sandler (1976) maintains, the therapist's emotional experience is most often an admixture of these two factors. Even when the therapist has a hunch that it is predominantly either his own issues or the patient's projective identification that is engendering his experience, it is always important to examine the alternative factor. This further inquiry is imperative and can be clearly illustrated by the example of a patient who is unconsciously attempting to arouse feelings of inadequacy in the therapist. Whereas one therapist might characteristically respond to such pressure with defensive arrogance, another might typically react with withdrawal, while a third might issue a masochistic invitation for the patient to redouble his efforts to depreciate. It is axiomatic that each therapist, through the benefit of personal analysis or psychotherapy as well as training, must learn to be aware of his tendencies or "personal equation" (Racker, 1953).

We propose five separate lines of inference, which represent vital checkpoints for the therapist in attempting to validate hypotheses regarding the source of his emotional response. They are: 1) What is observable in the interaction that may have contributed to the countertransference response? 2) Does there appear to be a correspondence between the therapist's experience of being with the patient and the patient's experience of being with the therapist? 3) Given a correspondence between the experiences of patient and therapist, does this role relationship appear in any way to be paradigmatic for the patient? 4) What else might be going on currently with the therapist that could be contributing to the experience of being with the patient? 5) Given a correspondence between the therapist's and the patient's experience, does this role relationship appear in any way to be paradigmatic for the therapist? In isolation, none of these areas of inquiry is sufficient to establish an adequate degree of confidence in the validity of a source hypothesis. To the extent that the therapist finds converging supportive evidence from these separate lines of inquiry, there will be an accompanying increase in confidence regarding the accuracy of the hypothesis. We now turn to a more systematic examination of the five lines of inference.

Line 1) What is observable in the interaction that may have contributed to the countertransference response? Once the therapist notes a countertransference response, it is very important to scrutinize the interaction as fully as possible in order to specify concrete features of the interaction that are associated with the particular response. There are times, of course, when certain major features are all too obvious, as in the case of the therapist who notes mounting irritation with a patient who is communicating in a hostile, sarcastic manner. However, even in such a situation, the therapist is ill advised to conclude the validating process with the assumption that the countertransference response is solely an outcome of the patient's projective identification. It may be that the patient's hostility represents an unconscious response to an accurate perception that the therapist has not been listening. This would place the matter in a much different light.

It may be that the therapist can point to nothing concrete in the interaction that seems to be prompting his response. The concrete aspects of the interaction may be too subtle to be detected, perhaps even with the assistance of supervision or consultation; or the therapist's response may emanate primarily from personal concerns. If, for example, a therapist consistently experiences sexual arousal with an attractive patient who in no apparent way acts seductively, it may be that the effects of a recent divorce in the life of the therapist is heavily influencing his reaction to the patient. Though not sufficient in the absence of other confirmatory evidence, the concrete data of the interaction are extremely important and useful in the validating process.

Line 2) Does there appear to be a correspondence between the therapist's experience of being with the patient and the patient's experience of being with the therapist? Though not essential, the hypothesis that a therapist's countertransference experience is influenced by a patient's projective identification is buttressed if a correspondence can be delineated between the experiences of patient and therapist. The Working Model and Empathic Connection subphases of our schema help to explicate the manner in which this correspondence may be determined. Such a correspondence may be either concordant or complementary in nature. The establishment of a correspondence in and of itself does not necessarily indicate that a patient's projective identification is at work.

For example, if a therapist is feeling impatient and annoyed with a patient and is able to establish that the patient, in complementary fashion, is feeling picked on, it is by no means sound to conclude that the therapist's hostility was induced by the patient's masochistic invitation, representing a reenactment of early childhood trauma. The role relationship *may be* such a form of reenactment induced by the patient's projective identification. It may also, however, be a consequence of the therapist's having a bad day and quite simply becoming impatient and insensitive with the patient; if projective identification is involved, it is the *therapist's* and not the patient's that is at work. It is also possible that the same role relationship represents a combination of these influences; that is, the patient could in fact be pressuring the therapist to become sadistic on a day when the therapist is unusually stressed, so that the therapist is unable to contain and interpret his own hostile impulses. To determine with any degree of confidence which of the three possibilities is actually unfolding, the therapist would need to search other lines of inference for convergence.

If the therapist is not able to ascertain any apparent correspondence between a countertransference response and the patient's experience, it suggests that his countertransference response emanates primarily from personal concerns that have little or nothing to do with the patient. For example, a therapist finds herself feeling desperately bored as she sits with an anorexic patient who has made excellent progress and whose eating habits have become quite normal. The therapist finds her thoughts wandering to other patients. She is puzzled by her response to the patient. She is able to detect no correspondence between her own experience of profound boredom and the experience of the patient, who seems quite lively and proud as she discusses the minutiae of recent meals—size of portions, quality of cooking, tastes and textures of different dishes, and the like.

It may be that the therapist is struggling with her own concerns around no longer feeling needed, and such a source hypothesis may in fact be borne out by subsequent investigation. Further exploration along other lines of inference could very well unearth a complementary role relationship that escaped notice when only the current interaction was being investigated. Subsequent experience with the patient may also substantiate an understanding of the role relationship as representing a reenactment for the patient of an early mother-child complementarity in which the child wishes the mother to love and admire all of her productions while, at the same time, the child fears that all attention will be lost to younger siblings who are "more in need."

Line 3) Given a correspondence between the experiences of patient and therapist, does this role relationship appear in any way to be paradigmatic for the patient? As we have alluded to, the mere determination of a correspondence between the experiences of patient and therapist in no way suffices to validate with adequate confidence the hypothesis that the source of the therapist's countertransference response emanates primarily from the patient's projective identification. An hypothesis unquestionably gathers support if the therapist can establish that the essential emotional features of the current patient-therapist experience of one another appear to echo important relationships both from the patient's past and from recent or ongoing involvements outside the therapy. The evidence becomes more compelling to the extent that the therapeutic interaction recapitulates a core repetitive pattern that destructively characterizes central and intimate relationships for the patient.

This discovery by no means exonerates the therapist from examining his own contribution. But in the presence of other supportive material, the establishment of a similarity between the current therapeutic role-relationship and the patient's experience of other significant relationships forcefully supports a source hypothesis that projective identification figures prominently in the countertransference response. Conversely, the absence of such evidence tends to refute the same hypothesis. With reference to our schema, the therapist will find that the utilization of the therapist-interaction working model and especially the patient-interaction working model will be useful in assessing this area.

As we emphasized in the Empathic Connection subphase, if in fact the correspondence between patient and therapist is complementary, there is frequently role reversal within the therapeutic setting. For example, a patient whose intimate relationships tend to be sadomasochistic in nature and whose prevailing core identification is on the masochistic side may nevertheless sadistically engender a masochistic countertransference response in the therapist.

Line 4) What else might be going on currently with the therapist that could be contributing to the experience of being with the patient? In both this and the following line of inference, the therapist seeks to examine his own contribution to the transference-countertransference experience. As we discussed in greater detail in the material examining disruptions in the empathic process, two influences on the therapist's personality organization come into play, both for better and for worse, that largely determine the extent of his contribution to the transference-countertransference experience. The first has to do with situational aspects of the therapist's current life adjustment; it represents the focus of this line of inference. It is vital that the therapist scrutinize a countertransference reaction for situational influences before leaping to the reckless conclusion that his countertransference response has been induced through the patient's projective identification.

The therapist must ask if having a particularly bad day could be the primary factor in his feeling unusual intolerance toward a patient. Conversely, is pleasure over some happy personal event inspiring a sense of good will toward a patient? Is an impending vacation engendering a struggle with abandonment guilt so that there is an attempt to please the patient? Financial concerns, marital problems, health problems, insufficient sleep, overwork, and the like can impinge upon the therapist's countertransference responsiveness in a major way and must be given serious consideration in attempting to validate a given source hypothesis. From the positive side of the therapist's current life adjustment, happy events such as marriage, the birth of a child or grandchild, the purchase of a new home, the publication of a paper, the excitement over an upcoming vacation, and the like can also exert a strong—and not always useful—influence on countertransference responsiveness.

In attempting to assess situational influences, the therapist must continuously take inventory of factors such as those that have been mentioned. It is also useful to question whether a given countertransference response resembles those that are occurring with other patients. For example, if a therapist finds that his attention is drifting with several consecutive patients, it is of course highly unlikely that his errant thoughts can be attributed to patient projective identification.

Line 5) Given a correspondence between the therapist's and the patient's experience, does this role relationship appear in any way to be paradigmatic for the therapist? In addition to exploring situational influences from the therapist's personal life that affect countertransference responsiveness, the therapist must also examine his own ongoing characterological makeup in an effort to avoid falsely attributing emotional responses to the influence of the patient's projective identification. It bears reemphasizing that it is critical for the therapist to be as aware as possible of his own "personal equation" (Racker, 1953). A male therapist's feeling of being unusually charmed by a female patient may have much more to do with the fact that she reminds him of a favorite sister than it has to do with the patient's projective identification. The therapist-interaction working model offers a valuable perspective for listening and for understanding the extent to which the therapist's own propensities are coming into play as the source of a given countertransference response. As Hoffman (1983) pointed out, the therapist is not an "empty container" of projective identifications any more than he is a blank screen for projections.

We should emphasize that responding in certain ways to a patient largely as a consequence of one's own personal concerns is by no means necessarily negative. However, it is virtually always problematic when the therapist is blind to the influence of his own inner world and essentially "blames" the patient for inducing a countertransference response that is difficult to manage. We all are aware of types of patients whom we find difficult. It is also essential to be aware of how one typically responds to certain presentations and styles of relating in patients. Does one typically respond to idealization with grandiosity, self-effacement, or annoyance? Does one respond stylistically to depreciation with withdrawal, retaliation, or becoming "too nice?" Self-examination with openness and the "suspension of superego criticism" (Fliess, 1942) is indispensable in validating the source of countertransference responses.

Having explored all five lines of inference pertaining to source hypotheses, the therapist is in a position to assess whether, and to what extent, there is sufficient convergence to validate whether a countertransference response is indeed a consequence of the patient's projective identification. If, on the contrary, personal concerns—whether situational or characterological—are predominantly responsible for the reaction to the patient, the therapist can then determine if this awareness helps to alleviate whatever treatment interferences might have been associated with the response in question. There are those occasions when this insight alone is insufficient to enable the therapist to work with "good enough" effectiveness. At such times, the standard recommendations for outside consultation or even additional treatment for the therapist are in fact well advised.

MEANING HYPOTHESES

Given that a therapist has validated the hypothesis with reasonable confidence that the patient's projective identification is at work in determining the countertransference response, the focus of attention then shifts to elucidating the meanings behind this role relationship and why it has occurred. *The effort to find meaning is best undertaken with the general hypothesis in mind that the patient, in some way or other, unconsciously needs the therapist to feel some form of what he is feeling and that this serves some purpose for the patient.*

To validate the hypothesis that a countertransference response has meaning for the patient, we propose five separate lines of inference from which, once again, the therapist may seek convergence. They include: 1) To what extent does the patient appear to be unconsciously re-creating, in the therapeutic relationship, the same pattern that has characterized prior intimate relationships? 2) In what ways does the patient's arousal of the therapist's countertransference response appear to represent a form of unconscious communication to the therapist? 3) To what extent does the patient's projective identification appear to be an unconscious response to a specific adaptive context (Langs, 1976) within the therapeutic interaction? 4) In what ways does the patient's projective identification appear to represent an attempt to rid the self of intolerable aspects? 5) Prior to an actual intervention, how is the therapist's countertransference response influenced by the silent hypothesis he has formulated regarding the meaning(s) for the patient of the countertransference response?

The therapist may immediately have a hunch that one of these areas of inquiry is especially salient, thus initiating the validating process along that particular line of inference. In the absence of such a hunch, there is no particular hierarchy of importance or rank order in which to pursue the validation of meaning hypotheses. As with the five lines of inference germane to source hypotheses, no single area of inquiry by itself suffices to establish an adequate degree of confidence in the validity of a meaning hypothesis. When there is sufficient convergence to establish reasonable validation of a meaning hypothesis, this validation itself provides additional support for the original source hypothesis that the patient's projective identification was indeed at work in arousing the countertransference response in question.

We will now proceed to a more thorough exploration of the five lines of inference pertaining to the hypothesis that the therapist's countertransference response is something that the patient unconsciously seeks.

Line 1) To what extent does the patient appear to be unconsciously re-creating, in the therapeutic relationship, the same pattern that has characterized prior intimate relationships? This line of inference overlaps considerably with the third line of inference in the validation of source hypotheses. The difference between these two lines of inference can be understood as follows. In the validation of source hypotheses, the criterion of "paradigmatic role-relationship" is used to confirm the location (within patient, therapist, or both) of the factors that contribute to the present countertransference reaction. In the validation of meaning hypotheses, the same criterion is used to confirm the patient's motivation to create a particular role relationship. By utilizing the therapist-interaction and especially the patient-interaction working models, the therapist attempts to ascertain similarities between the patient-therapist experience and other intimate relationships, both past and present, that the patient has experienced. As totalist countertransference theory has demonstrated, it is to be expected that the patient's characteristic problems in human relationships—what Racker (1957) has referred to as the patient's "vicious circle"—will likely be repeated, sooner or later, in some form in the therapeutic interaction. As we have emphasized, this paradigmatic interaction may be either concordant or complementary in nature, with or without role reversal from the manner in which the pattern customarily unfolds for the patient in his relationships with others.

The important question arises as to whether or not this recreation of the past in the present through the mechanism of projective identification is unconsciously motivated. We maintain that this question must be answered in the affirmative. Intrapsychic character structure comes into formation as a consequence of defenses and adaptations by which the individual unconsciously attempts to deal with wishes, fears, impulses, frustrations, gratifications, and anxieties. The defenses and adaptations within an individual's character structure are a consequence of the unconscious motivation to seek pleasure and avoid pain. Motivated intrapsychic character structure is then reflected in the manner in which an individual interacts with others. For example, if a person's core experiences in intimate interpersonal relationships have been characterized by exploitation and abuse, there is a strong likelihood of a repetition compulsion to reenact this same experience over and over. There are those who would argue that the repetitive pattern comes as a consequence not of unconscious motivation but of developmental deficit and fixation, such that the person is simply incapable of interacting in any other fashion. But this style of interacting may very well elicit from others the behavior that conforms to the expectation that others are not to be trusted. Similarly, a masochistic person, by means of projective identification, tends to arouse sadistic behavior from others—or, at the very least, behavior that could plausibly be *construed* by the patient as sadistic.

Although he does not use the term projective identification, Schafer (1984) suggests that the underlying motivation for such repetitive styles of interacting is very often unconsciously designed to "pursue" the very form of "failure" that manifestly makes the individual so miserable. In describing the dynamics of self-fulfilling prophesy, Schafer asserts that the underlying motivation behind what we refer to as projective identification can in fact be highly specific, as opposed to the more global level of motivation that is generally associated with enduring character structure. Schafer emphasizes that in "failing," the individual may actually succeed, for example, in remaining loyal to a critical parent.

The therapist gathers support that the patient does in fact have an unconscious stake in arousing the therapist's countertransference response to the extent that he is able to delineate similarities between the patient-therapist relationship and other core relationships for the patient—especially those with parents, spouses, and other family members. Although not sufficient in itself to validate a meaning hypothesis, this line of inference can then be compared with evidence from other lines.

Line 2) In what way does the patient's arousal of the therapist's countertransference response appear to represent a form of unconscious communication to the therapist? We agree with both Ogden (1979) and Grotstein (1981) that projective identification represents a compelling form of communication that is potentially much more powerful than words alone. In attempting to determine and validate the meaning for the patient of a particular countertransference response, we have emphasized throughout this volume that the patient may in fact be communicating to the therapist something about his own emotional experience, past or present, or about his experience of his objects.

Returning to the question of motivation considered in the previous line of inference, we regard as moot whether or not a patient is in fact motivated, consciously or unconsciously, to make this form of communication through projective identification. In the previous line of inference, we proposed that unconscious defensive motivation is always present at a global level with respect to enduring character structure and the accompanying repetitive styles of interacting, in which repetition compulsion and projective identification play a part. The same cannot be said of underlying motivation with regard to the communicative aspect of projective identification.

For example, a patient who feels controlled by the therapist may unconsciously attempt to master resultant anxiety by turning the tables on the therapist by means of projective identification, thus making the therapist feel controlled and thereby restoring to himself a sense of being in the driver's seat. In this scenario, the patient is not necessarily also attempting unconsciously to communicate to the therapist how it felt to be controlled so that the therapist could then comprehend the patient's experience in a more vivid way. Upon exploration, it may be decided that the communicative motivation is present, but it cannot be assumed to exist. In a global sense, it could be argued that the patient came to therapy in the first place to seek help through the therapist's understanding. But it does not necessarily follow that the patient is unconsciously seeking to communicate to the therapist in a *specific instance* of projective identification. The projective identification may be motivated unconsciously only by an effort to master an anxiety-provoking situation by turning passive into active. The existence of an unconscious communicative motivation may be present, but this cannot automatically be assumed.

We are stressing this point not so much because of its theoretical interest, but because it has important clinical ramifications. It can be infuriating to a patient who is expressing anger toward a therapist for the therapist to applaud the patient's expression of anger. Similarly, if a therapist suggests that a patient is trying to engage in useful communication when the patient is aware only of a wish to retaliate, the patient may well feel patronized and be even more disturbed with the therapist.

But whether or not the patient is unconsciously motivated to communicate to the therapist by means of projective identification, far and away the more important point is that the in-

teraction represents a rich opportunity for the therapist to understand something very vividly about the patient's experience, whether or not the patient unconsciously intended this communication to occur. To the extent that the therapist is able to recognize similarities between a countertransference experience and the experience of either the patient or the patient's objects, support is built for the countertransference response having communicative meaning for the patient, whether or not the position is taken that unconscious motivation is involved.

Line 3) To what extent does the patient's projective identification appear to be an unconscious response to a specific adaptive context within the therapeutic interaction? Langs's (1976) term "adaptive context" refers to any event in the treatment situation to which the patient must adapt. The event, or stimulus, may be as uncommon for the patient as impending termination or the therapist's forgetting an appointment, or as common as a therapist's intervention or silence. In attempting to formulate and validate the meaning of a particular countertransference response, it is useful to explore the extent to which the patient may be engaging in projective identification as a consequence of something very specific in the therapist's activity. For example, if a patient is feeling exploited by a therapist's raising his fee, the patient may respond in either of two ways: he may subtly maneuver the therapist into feeling abused himself, or he may respond in such a way as to provoke feelings of guilt, greed, and exploitiveness within the therapist. The ensuing countertransference response will depend on the therapist's capacity to absorb this influence.

Though insufficient by itself to establish that a patient does indeed have an unconscious purpose in arousing the particular countertransference response, the meaning hypothesis is supported by the finding of a potential connection between the countertransference response and a patient's efforts to adapt to some event or stimulus within the therapeutic interaction.

Line 4) In what ways does the patient's projective identification appear to represent an attempt to rid the self of intolerable aspects? Melanie Klein (1946) introduced the term projective identification to refer to an intrapsychic mechanism of defense in which intolerable affects were managed through the fantasy of these affects being projected into the mental representation of an internalized object. Klein herself did not regard the external object, including the therapist in the clinical situation, as being influenced. But extension of the term into the interpersonal realm requires the therapist to consider that the given countertransference response may represent an unconscious effort by the patient to have the therapist "contain" or "metabolize" aspects of self that the patient experiences as intolerable. The interpersonal manifestations of projective identification, as we have been emphasizing, are by no means limited to ridding the self of intolerable aspects. Nevertheless, this is an important option to consider in determining the underlying meaning of a countertransference response. A patient who is furious with a therapist, but who finds rage intolerable to experience, may then succeed in inducing this experience of intense anger within the therapist, allowing the patient the more comfortable and familiar role of victim.

This same phenomenon may also occur in relation to outside figures. For example, a patient with severe self-esteem problems describes to her therapist a recent dinner with her father at which the father reportedly commented on how fat his daughter looked. The patient relates all of this in a very matter-of-fact way, as though speaking of the weather. The therapist notes within himself mounting anger at what he experiences as the appalling and destructive insensitivity of the father, even as the patient states that she feels "nothing . . . only numbness" toward father.

Line 5) Prior to an actual intervention, how is the therapist's countertransference response influenced by the silent hypothesis he has formulated regarding the meaning(s) for the patient of the countertransference response? The following countertransference features tend to be supportive of the underlying source and meaning hypotheses.

First, validating support for a meaning hypothesis is provided by the therapist's sense of enhanced cognitive and affective understanding of the interaction and the intricacy of the patient's dynamics, which sets the therapeutic interaction into a more predictable context. The task for the therapist is clearer. The formulation of a valid meaning hypothesis should help to explain how and why certain feelings are arising in the present interaction. Following the development of a tentative hypothesis, there is often the experience of several subtle, perhaps seemingly minor, aspects of the interaction suddenly "making sense" or falling into line with the proposed understanding of how the two participants are engaged in a mutually defined pattern of interaction.

Second, an accurate formulation of the meaning behind the current correspondence between experiential states often produces a feeling of relief and increased objective distance from the intensity of the therapist's introjective identification. The improved level of comfort and greater observational capacity within the therapist may be rapid in their onset or develop slowly over time as the therapist works through the underlying issues with the patient. The general feeling of relief is accompanied by an improvement in the therapist's cognitive functioning, which may have been diminished during the initial uncomfortable experience of the identification. Improved confidence and a heightened sense of security renders the therapist less defensive. An atmosphere of what might be confusion and turbulence tends to be replaced by a sense of calmness and clarity. The therapist may experience the feelings of pride in a job well done and a renewed sense of hopefulness concerning the treatment of the patient.

Third, a hypothesis that adequately addresses the correspondence between the participants' emotional states often increases the therapist's receptivity to the patient's influence. With a firmer grip on the role the patient is attempting to assign to him, the therapist is less apt to shut off interactional pressure out of defensive feelings of discomfort. The therapist knows more about the type of information he is looking for. This fresh approach to the countertransference-transference encounter is necessary to deepen the exploration and awareness of the introjective identification rather than to resist it. The renewed sensitivity within the therapist is reminiscent of the "second wind" phenomenon experienced by athletes.

Fourth, there may be a reduction in negative affect (e.g., anger, boredom, impatience) toward the patient and an increase in appreciation for the patient's need to communicate through the immediate interpersonal channels. In those countertransference reactions which involved highly positive affects, such as idealization of the patient, there will likely be a similar moderating influence. When the struggle over processing an identification no longer occupies center stage, the therapist will notice that the patient's needs can be returned to the central focus of awareness. The therapist can better discern and accept the reasons a patient has constructed the role relationship in a particular manner. In short, the therapist will experience an increase in his overall empathic appreciation of the patient.

Finally, a frequent byproduct of arriving at an accurate hypothesis is that the therapist knows more about himself. In arriving at a formulation, the therapist has been forced to examine the involvement of his own personal equation (Racker, 1957) in the countertransference reaction. A meaning hypothesis that is on target will shed additional light on the unique features of the therapist's personality makeup as he responds to interactional pressure from the patient. The enhancement of self-understanding for the therapist has the potential to generalize outside of the treatment setting.

POSTINTERVENTION VALIDATION

The two levels—source and meaning—of validating hypotheses concerning countertransference responses that we have delineated both involve only internal processing by the therapist. Nothing has been said about the validating process once an actual intervention, and especially an interpretation, has been made. The subject of validating an interpretation on the basis of a patient's subsequent responses has been taken up elsewhere in the literature. In brief, we are in agreement with such criteria as: the emergence of new material that makes unconscious motives and defenses more intelligible (Freud, 1913; Hendrick, 1950; Isaacs, 1939; Kubie, 1952; Langs, 1976), enhanced self-understanding for the patient (Alexander, 1935; Erikson, 1958; Ricoeur, 1977; Rychlak, 1968), enhanced communication between patient and therapist (Erikson, 1958; Langs, 1976), and the appearance of derivatives in the patient's material referring to positive introjects (French, 1958; Langs, 1976, 1978). These postintervention validating criteria themselves should be subjected to the principle of converging lines of inference. However, because they are transference-based criteria, this undertaking is outside the scope of the present volume.

With regard to the countertransference-based validating process as it continues once an intervention has been made, the timing and the technical facility of the intervention is at least as important as its content. This subject is taken up in greater detail in the material on the Communication phase of the empathic process (see chapter 7). As a consequence, it may well be that the underlying source and meaning hypotheses are reasonably valid, but the nature of their delivery in the therapist's intervention produces untoward results that belie the accuracy of the content. The patient may feel shocked, confused, criticized, humiliated, or misunderstood to a degree that may be highly disruptive to the treatment process. Such a response would then have obvious consequences for the therapist's ensuing countertransference attitude. This possibility needs to be considered with respect to the therapist's ongoing scrutiny of his own emotional experience of the patient as a barometer of the validity of source and meaning hypotheses.

If we can assume good timing and technique in the delivery of a countertransference-based intervention—and this is a major assumption, indeed—the therapist finds evidence to support the validity of the underlying source and meaning hypotheses if his ongoing countertransference attitude tends to be characterized by the features that were delineated in the fifth line of inference for meaning hypotheses. Although this list is by no means exhaustive, when these features are present, the therapist's confidence level in the validity of his formulations rises.

In summary, several overall points should be mentioned. First, nonconfirmatory criteria in the validation of a source or meaning hypothesis are characterized by the absence of convergence among the lines of inference cited earlier or by the presence of material that directly opposes these positive criteria. For example, following the formulation of a meaning hypothesis, the therapist may experience increased confusion, intensification of the uncomfortable identification, decreased receptivity to the patient's communication efforts, reduction in appreciation of the patient's motivations, or little or no insight into his own personality makeup. But if the therapist is to take advantage of either positive or negative validating criteria, he must be attuned to his internal reactions. The therapist who remains defensively entrenched will not be in a position to evaluate the emotional signals of confirmation or disconfirmation available to him.

Second, the validating process, like the empathic process, has no true endpoint. It is an ongoing undertaking involving progressive levels of depth, refinement, and elaboration as the "truth of the matter" between patient and therapist is illuminated. Even as the therapist arrives at the level of postintervention validation, the stage is being set for recycling the same process all over again, with similar or new material. Though we cannot hope to achieve airtight proofs of our clinical hypotheses, the preintervention and postintervention lines of inference we have outlined, in keeping with the principle of convergence, provide the therapist with potential guidelines.

Finally, as in other segments of this volume, when presenting a detailed examination of complex internal processes we run the risk of seeming to suggest that the therapist should be consciously aware of all validating criteria at all times and be able to assess them completely within the immediate interaction with the patient. To the contrary, the countertransference reaction is usually more easily analyzed between sessions or over several sessions, when the interactional pressure is lightened. The time frame for the validation process can range from the immediate moment to several weeks or months. The clinical illustrations described in chapter 10 present examples of varying time frames for the development, analysis, and validation of countertransference reactions.

9 *Countertransference Disclosure*

USES AND ABUSES

The subject of countertransference disclosure is an important, complex, and highly debated matter. The passion that is brought to this debate is best understood as an historical outgrowth of earlier disagreements about the existence and usefulness of countertransference material. The question of disclosure to the patient of the therapist's experience of the therapeutic interaction challenges both theoretical and technical understandings of the therapeutic process. In the present chapter, we shall review the central issues of countertransference disclosure, their evolution over time, and the accompanying theoretical and technical implications. Finally, we shall present criteria that can be helpful to the clinician in distinguishing between useful and disruptive communications of countertransference material.

As stated in chapter 2, countertransference theory has progressed through three distinct stages. Initially, countertransference reactions of the therapist had to be acknowledged as inevitable. Once this had occurred, it became possible to recognize the potential usefulness of countertransference reactions in understanding the experience of the patient. More recently there has been an effort to classify countertransference material as to type and possible correspondence to internalized object relational paradigms of the patient. A predictable outgrowth of this progression is the question of whether or not the actual communication to the patient of the therapist's experience within the therapeutic interaction increases the therapeutic action of the treatment process. In this context, disclosure of countertransference is an extension of the utilization of countertransference reactions initiated in the 1950s.

Despite countertransference theory having become a subject of increasing interest, surprisingly little has been written about disclosure. Resistance to any degree of countertransference disclosure seems to rest on both personal and theoretical grounds. From a personal point of view, therapists can be understandably reluctant to acknowledge to themselves—let alone to their patients—the strong emotional reactions that can be elicited in the therapeutic interaction. This is especially true when powerful negative emotions are experienced toward the patient. In any context, such emotions may be difficult to tolerate and manage. But in the therapeutic interaction, the therapist has the additional burden of his role as a professional, within which it is easy to fall into a belief that one should not be influenced by strong emotions.

Hesitance to countertransference disclosure also arises on theoretical grounds, since it seemingly contradicts the concept of neutrality and the rule of abstinence. To some extent, the psychoanalytic therapist continues to labor under the misguided notion that he is a "blank screen" upon which projections of the patient's transference are analyzed (Hoffman, 1983). This rationale holds that the "real" experience of the therapist, if disclosed to the patient, can only contaminate the sterile field into which the patient projects his intrapsychic conflicts. Furthermore, the blank screen therapist, like the surgeon (Freud, 1912), is required to put all his own feelings aside in the interest of "objective" attention to the patient's material. The classical, drive-based formulation of the treatment process has dramatically shifted since Freud's early recommendations.

The shift has been accompanied by alternative understandings of the role of the therapist's reactions. As the treatment process has come to be seen as a complex interplay of projective and introjective mechanisms in which the experience of the therapist is central to the therapeutic process, the clinical application of technical neutrality has had to be reconsidered.

As the acknowledgment of countertransference has gained ascendance within the field, the concept of neutrality has shifted from the prescription that the therapist occupy the role of blank screen. In its place has come the warning to the therapist that he not let his own reactions find expression in the interaction with the patient. Thus, a therapist may very well experience any of a multitude of strong reactions in response to a patient, but these feelings should be barred from interfering with the therapist's "neutral," controlled composure while he is in actual interaction with the patient. Neutrality in this second application refers to restraint and control over whatever emotional state is experienced by the therapist.

A third application of neutrality allows the therapist to communicate his emotional experience of the interaction to the patient, but the therapist's communications are to be expressed in a tone and content that reflect mastery and "objectivity" (Winnicott, 1949) over his emotional reaction. This interpretation of neutrality demonstrates an effort to adhere to the important tenets of classical psychoanalytic theory while at the same time incorporating changes in technical and theoretical assumptions.

Most authors have entirely avoided the complex issue of when, how much, and in what form the countertransference experience should or should not be communicated to the patient, a reluctance that reflects the "near phobic dread of this area of technique within psychoanalysis" (Bollas, 1983, p. 30). But in regard to those who have written on the subject, a review of the literature reveals three basic positions in regard to the disclosure of countertransference. Taken together, they represent a continuum ranging from total abstinence, to utilization at highly selective points in treatment, and finally to more active and continuous usage of explicit countertransference material.

THE CONSERVATIVE PERSPECTIVE

The conservative position is illustrated by the writings of Heimann (1950), Langs, (1978), and Annie Reich (1960). Both Heimann and Langs argued that the therapist's awareness of his own experience can be a useful tool in understanding the experience of the patient. Nevertheless, they concluded that direct communication from the therapist concerning his experience of the interaction burdens the patient unnecessarily. Communications of the countertransference result in the therapist's simply discharging his own unresolved transferences into the therapuetic interaction and shifting the focus of the therapeutic work away from the patient's experience. As Heimann wrote:

> . . . I do not consider it right for the analyst to communicate his feelings to his patient. In my view such honesty is more in the nature of a confession and a burden to the patient. In any case it leads away from the analysis. The emotions roused in the analyst will be of value to this patient, if used as one more source of insight into the patient's unconscious conflicts and defenses; and when these are interpreted and worked through, the ensuing changes in the patient's ego include the strengthening of his reality sense so that he sees his analyst as a human being, not a god or a demon, and the "human" relationship in the analytic situation follows without the analyst having recourse to extra-analytical means [p. 84].

Langs (1978) took a similar stand against the therapist's self-revelation, even if the disclosure is based on "noncountertransference." (Langs retained the narrow definition of countertransference as pathological.) But in addition to burdening the patient, he emphasized the resultant alteration in the "framework" of the treatment, which he regarded as pathologically counterproductive.

Although Reich (1960) disagreed with Heimann and Langs that strong emotional reactions on the therapist's part could be useful, she nevertheless agreed that countertransference material should not be disclosed. She criticized the mention of countertransference reactions as an attempt to bypass the psychoanalytic method of interpretation by substituting transference gratifications in an effort to supply healthier identificatory models:

> Some authors advocate the free expression of countertransference feelings, including negative ones, as a method designed to promote identification by the patient with the healthier personality of the analyst. For instance, Little (1951) deems it necessary for very disturbed patients to experience the analyst as a loving, hating, feeling person and to introject him, so that they themselves may become capable of feeling. Identification with the analyst is viewed by numerous authors as one of the main vehicles of therapy also for patients with less serious disturbances . . . . It is not the aim of analysis to transform these temporary identifications into permanent structures . . . . They need not be promoted by any "acting out" on the part of the analyst, which can result—in the most favorable case—in some educational impact upon the patient, but not in his being analyzed [p. 393].

THE MODERATE PERSPECTIVE

A second, more tolerant stance toward countertransference disclosure has been taken by a moderate group that believes that countertransference disclosure should be judiciously employed, but only on an infrequent basis. Various justifications offered for the therapist's self-revelation include the acknowledgment of an error (Giovacchini, 1972b; Greenson, 1974) and the navigation of a therapeutic impasse or crisis (Giovacchini, 1972b; Winnicott, 1949).

In addition, Winnicott (1949) maintained that well-timed countertransference disclosure in working with seriously disturbed patients serves the needs of both patient and therapist. He believed that patients' developmental needs could be met more effectively by allowing them to "reach" the therapist's "objective hate" as a prerequisite to reaching the therapist's "objective love" (p. 72). For the therapist, Winnicott emphasized the need to discharge negative feelings for the patient in a controlled manner so as to continue to tolerate the patient under the stressful circumstances which the patient induces:

> The important thing is that each time just as I put him outside the door, I told him something; I said that what had happened had made me hate him. This was easy because it was true . . . . I think these words were important from the point of view of progress, but they were mainly important in enabling me to tolerate the situation without letting out, without losing my temper and every now and again murdering him [p. 73].

With regard to severely character disordered patients, Giovacchini (1972b) addressed several potential benefits for the patient of countertransference disclosure. In addition to providing validation to the patient that his perceptions may be accurate, it also allows the patient the opportunity to observe the therapist as he applies the analytic method to himself in an effort to promote clarity and honesty within the therapeutic interaction. Giovacchini emphasized that countertransference disclosure, if properly handled, may enable therapist and patient to address what may be crucial elements of reenactment within the therapy of past traumatic situations and conflicts. From such a disclosure, it could be possible to understand more fully the ways in which the patient in fact may have needed to induce this particular feeling state within the therapist. An earlier version of this point was intimated in the work of Berman (1949), one of the first to favor countertransference disclosure as an effort to contend with certain distancing operations of the patient.

Despite the emphasis on discretion in selecting the proper time for countertransference disclosure, the moderate group does not rigorously clarify criteria for useful disclosures versus those which burden the patient. Nevertheless, the moderates clearly differentiate themselves from the conservatives, who essentially dodge this question by maintaining that explicit self-revelation by the therapist should play no part in psychoanalytic treatment.

THE RADICAL PERSPECTIVE

A third, more radical group of authors takes the position that countertransference disclosure is a customary element of the therapist's daily repertoire. Although the need for discretion is frequently mentioned, the radical group holds that countertransference disclosure is a necessary technical tool that does not have to be justified by intense affect within the therapist, staunch resistance within the patient, or a seemingly insurmountable impasse or crisis in the therapy relationship.

Little (1951, 1957) was the first advocate of this position. Citing the usefulness of expressing the therapist's "real feeling" for the patient, she believed that prudent countertransference disclosure actually paves the way for transference interpretations:

> Let me make it clear that I do not mean that I think countertransference interpretations should be unloaded injudiciously without consideration on the heads of hapless patients, any more than transference interpretation are given without thought today. I mean that they should neither be positively avoided or perhaps restricted to feelings which are justified or objective, such as those to which Dr. Winnicott refers in his paper on "Hate on the Countertransference" (*International Journal of Psychoanalysis,* 1949). (And of course they cannot be given unless something of the countertransference has become conscious.) The subjectivity of the feelings needs to be shown to the patient, though their actual origin need not be gone into (there should not be confessions); . . . In my view a time comes in the course of every analysis when it is essential for the patient to recognize the existence not only of the analyst's objective or justified feelings, but also of the analyst's subjective feelings (1951, p. 38).

Tauber (1954) went so far as to advocate disclosure of the therapist's own dream material to the patient as a method of stimulating the analytic process. Like the other radical proponents of explicit countertransference revelation, he believed that both patient and analyst need to surmount the "taboo" against countertransference material in order to provide a "constant infusion of new materials, fresh appraisals, and a challenging reconsideration of issues in the light of provocative data" (p. 332). Although he too warned against the dangers of acting out with the patient, he believed that the prohibition against divulging explicit countertransference material could result in stagnation such that "the so-called standardization of the procedure and the established scientific postulates can themselves become targets of the patient's resistance" (p. 332).

Searles (1965) is perhaps the most widely published proponent of the radical position, at times conveying an aggressive stance toward the use of the therapist's subjective state in the therapeutic process:

> I find a generous place in psychotherapy for all the sadism I can muster—for example, to needle and infuriate the apathetic or out of contact patient into more overt relatedness, or to pay him back for the hurts he has been inflicting upon me. With an abundance of this kind

> of interaction between us, he has good reason to know that I am in no wise a saint, and we can deal with his own problems about sadism in a person to person fashion . . . . Surely it is no coincidence that, as I have become relatively comfortable with feelings of adoring and being adored, I have become much freer to express and make therapeutic use of previously suppressed scornful feelings toward patients, finding that these do not destroy, but rather help to activate the therapeutic relatedness [pp. 25–26].

Although these passages seem to indicate that he accepted no limitations on what is permissable to disclose to a patient, Searles (1975) did in fact restrict his self-revelations to those reactions which are in direct response to the interaction with the patient. The line is drawn short of any disclosure conveying personal material relating to the therapist's past or present life outside of the therapeutic interaction.

Among current authors, Bollas (1983) is an articulate spokesman for the more radical perspective on countertransference disclosure. Formulating the interactive process between therapist and patient in Winnicottian terms, he emphasizes the therapist's subjective experience as a crucial source of free association, which must begin with the therapist before it can occur for the patient. One of the therapist's primary tasks is to understand the meaning of his own experience in relationship to the patient and to place that meaning into the "potential space" between analyst and patient for a collaborative analysis. The therapist must develop the capacity to assume a temporary "process identity" resulting from the interactional influence of the patient and the therapist's "generative countertransference regression":

> Because the analyst is the Other patient, sustaining in himself some intersubjective discourse with the analysand, it is essential to find some way to put forward for analytic investigation that which is occurring in the analyst as a purely subjective and private experience. It is essential to do this because in many patients the truly free associative process takes place within the analyst, and the clinician must find some way to report his internal processes thereby linking the patient with something he has lost in himself and enabling him to engage more authentically with the free associative process [p. 6].

The radical perspective of countertransference disclosure holds that there are both potential benefits and dangers for the therapeutic process. On the positive side, the strong accent on the therapist's active and continuous use of his subjective experience in formulating explicit interventions seems to foster greater and more consistent self-awareness for the therapist, since his subjective experience is viewed as a constant source of data. For the patient, when this approach is properly implemented, there is perhaps less risk of viewing the therapist as an authoritarian, superior, or godlike figure over time. Through the therapist's self-disclosure, the impact a patient has on others—not just the therapist—may possibly be illuminated more clearly, thereby enriching the potential for insight, understanding, and resolution.

And yet the dangers of active countertransference disclosure must also be respected. For the therapist, the question of validation is paramount. Simply because he happens to feel bored, for example, with a particular patient does not by itself necessarily reflect anything meaningful about the patient. And if it does, it may still not be useful to disclose that to the patient. Furthermore, simply because a therapist is self-disclosive does not guarantee that the patient will be more apt to see him as a more "real," less idealized, or less authoritarian figure. In part, the patient's perception of the therapist depends on the patient's character structure. But it is also true that a therapist can be self-disclosive in a highly insistent and authoritarian manner, which might perpetuate or reinforce a patient's idealization of the analyst as omniscient.

There are no clear guidelines presented by any of the three positions—unless one takes the position of total abstinence as a guideline. In the following section, we attempt to differentiate the characteristics of explicit countertransference-based interventions that are useful and productive from those which are disruptive and counterproductive. We do so with the recognition that any clinical situation is very complex. The mechanical imposition of rigid guidelines is no substitute for sound clinical judgment. The guidelines we propose are intended to enhance clinical judgment, not to replace it.

With reference to the Communication phase of our schema, we have discriminated two forms of intervention that build upon countertransference material—those interventions which explicitly refer only to countertransference material and those which refer both to countertransference and transference material (see chapter 7). The guidelines that follow are an attempt to clarify the potential risks and rewards of those two types of interventions, as well as to consider various underlying technical considerations.

The therapist must always work toward analyzing and understanding the nature of the interaction between himself and his patient rather than merely engaging in a pattern of action and reaction. The latter occurrence typically represents a blind reenactment with the patient of a vicious circle in human relationships. The patient's repetitive pattern is then played out with the therapist rather than usefully examined. This danger is especially prevalent in the explicit use of countertransference material to a patient. At the same time, productive use of a countertransference-based intervention provides an additional therapeutic resource that can be enormously potent from the point of view of interrupting and interpreting the patient's vicious circle in human relationships.

In attempting to differentiate those countertransference-based interventions that are useful from those which are not, we shall adopt a before-during-after orientation, examining the preparation, implementation, and impact of those interventions which explicitly refer to the therapist's experience.

THE PREPARATION OF A COUNTERTRANSFERENCE-BASED INTERVENTION

The preparation of a useful countertransference-based intervention has several components. With reference to our schema, the therapist must have completed all of the tasks of the Reception subphase, including properly focused attention to the patient and to the interaction, sufficient receptivity to the patient's interactional pressure by which the projective identification is induced, and a recognition of the concomitant signal affect as an indicator that an identification has indeed taken place. With these accomplishments as a foundation, the therapist is then in a position to move into the vitally important and often difficult subphases of Internal Processing.

The subphase of Containment-Separateness is the area in which breakdowns are most likely to occur in the preparation of any intervention, but especially those which are countertransference-based, primarily because of the tendency to react to, rather than investigate, the induced identifications. Even if the therapist remains fully conscious of the signal affect associated with the particular identification that has been induced and does not have to resort to defensive operations, it can still be very difficult to separate oneself sufficiently from what one is experiencing in order to begin to observe and analyze the nature of the interaction that has developed.

Following Greenson (1960) and Fliess (1942), we have delineated some of the intrapsychic features necessary for the therapist to establish sufficient psychological distance from an induced identification (Tansey and Burke, 1985). These include a suspension of superego criticism in order to tolerate what may seem to be objectionable feelings toward a patient or oneself (for example, revulsion, sexual arousal, hopelessness, incompetence), a firm realization that the identification is temporary in nature, and the stability of personality organization that enables the therapist to realize that his current experience of self, however uncomfortable, does not constitute an unmanageable threat to self-esteem. It goes without saying that a therapist generally is able to handle these tasks more effectively with those identifications that do not touch on sensitive areas of unresolved conflict or personal vulnerability.

A therapist, for example, who feels irritated by a patient's ridicule must gain a grip on himself before he can hope to intervene usefully. By listening to this material through the therapist-interaction working model, he may feel that he is in a position to make either an explicit countertransference-based intervention ("You know, for some reason I am finding myself feeling impatient with you today and I believe this would be useful for us to try to understand") or an implicit countertransference-based intervention using the same material ("You seem to me to be looking for an argument today. Any ideas what this might be all about?"). As will be discussed further in our examination of the implementation of an intervention, either intervention can be offered in a way that invites productive analysis; at the same time, either intervention might be construed by the patient as an actualization and enactment of the very scenario the therapist is purporting to examine. If the therapist intervenes in what seems to the patient to be an irritated tone of voice, then the intervention may come across as a form of blame or retaliation. An unfavorable outcome will be much less likely, though still possible, if the therapist has separated himself sufficiently from the induced identification to intervene in a calm and evenhanded manner.

Second, in preparing a countertransference-based intervention, it is extremely important that the therapist pay particular attention to how he expects the patient to receive the intervention. It is in this area that the therapist internally processes the proposed intervention in a future-oriented manner within the working model and empathic connection subphases. Through the patient-interaction working model, the therapist draws on his past experience with the patient to use countertransference-based interventions in determining the form and depth of his communication to the patient.

Bollas (1983) distinguished between "indirect" and "direct" use of the countertransference. The former refers to the therapist's communicating something to the patient about his subjective "sense of the situation," including such things as "hunches," whether or not he discloses feelings related to the patient. Direct use of the countertransference is characterized by "declaring more clearly how one feels to be the object of the patient's transference" (p. 12). He suggests that indirect countertransference-based interventions often serve as useful groundwork for the more ambitious direct countertransference-based interventions.

Similarly, we maintain that a transference-based interpretation often has a less jarring effect on a patient and is frequently easier to digest and utilize than a countertransference-based interpretation. For example, a patient may be receptive to a transference-based interpretation designed to illuminate the patient's possible underlying wish to destroy the therapist's care and concern. Such an interpretation may be more useful than a countertransference-based interpretation that discloses the therapist's mounting feelings of boredom, since the latter has considerable potential to shock the patient without preliminary groundwork. As with any clinical guideline, however, there are exceptions depending on the patient, the therapist, the status of the interaction, and the timing and accuracy of the transference interpretation. In general, a therapist who is considering a countertransference-based interpretation is on firmer ground with a patient who has been able to work well with transference-based interpretations.

A third critical aspect in the preparation of a countertransference-based intervention has to do with the therapist's motivation for advancing the interpretation. Optimally, any such interpretation is offered in a spirit of attempting to understand an important aspect of the patient. The therapist puts forth some elements of what he is experiencing as a means toward that end. In an ill-prepared countertransference-based intervention, the therapist may be more powerfully motivated by a wish to retaliate or to discharge the impulses associated with the induced identification. He may feel unwilling or unable to serve as the repository or container (Bion, 1959) of the induced indentification. The countertransferenced-based intervention is then motivated not so much by a wish to understand the patient as by a need for relief by enacting the identification or "dumping" it back into the patient's lap. The problem becomes more serious to the degree that the therapist himself is blind to the darker side of his underlying motivation. Although there are no foolproof indicators of insufficient self-awareness in the therapist's preparation of a countertransference-based intervention, he needs to be cautious about intervening with this kind of potent material when he notes in himself such qualities as agitation, excitement, pressure, and the like. Such a feeling state strongly suggests that further self-scrutiny is warranted before utilization of a countertransference-based intervention.

THE IMPLEMENTATION OF A COUNTERTRANSFERENCE-BASED INTERVENTION

By implementation, we are referring to all that occurs in the delivery of an intervention, including such factors as timing, tact, tone of voice, language and wording, as well as whether the intervention is ambitious or more tentative and involves an explicit or implicit use of countertransference. With regard to our overall schema, matters of implementation are accounted for in the Communication phase.

When a therapist is well-prepared to advance a countertransference-based intervention, this is very often clearly reflected in tone of voice and choice of language. Especially in those situations in which the content of the interpretation involves strong emotions, it is critical that the interpretation be delivered in an evenhanded manner. This is not to say that the tone needs to be devoid of color or animation in the name of "neutrality," since a quality of stiffness or unemotionality can itself represent an enactment of remoteness and emotional uninvolvement that warrants further examination. Rather, we are suggesting that care be exercised to ensure that the achievement of sufficient psychological distance from the induced identification is in fact reflected in the presentation of the interpretation, especially in one that is countertransference-based.

If, for example, a therapist says to a patient, "You know, I feel as though nothing I say to you today is going to feel useful to you" in an annoyed, depressed, or critical tone of voice, the impact will likely be unfavorable. The patient will be much more apt to experience the therapist as merely reacting, rather than attempting to investigate something potentially significant. Even when such an intervention is accompanied by a tone of concern or curiosity, the patient may still experience it as hostile, but the chances of this happening are reduced to the extent that the therapist does not simply *discharge* frustration in his efforts to *examine* the potential meaningfulness of his frustrated condition. The same guidelines hold for tactfulness and the selection of language in the implementation of an intervention, since those elements of intervention also can reflect an enactment of the very self-state the therapist is attempting to offer to the patient for collaborative examination.

As we have already mentioned, in a well-implemented countertransferenced-based intervention, the therapist is inviting a patient to join in examing what the therapist is subjectively experiencing, because of the possible consequences which this collaboration might hold for understanding the patient himself. Both Bollas (1983) and Ogden (1985) cite Winnicott (1971) in referring to any intervention, whether or not it utilizes countertransference material, as the therapist's placing something into the "potential space" between himself and the patient. There is then the opportunity for the intervention to be "played with—kicked around, mulled over, torn to pieces—rather than regarded as other versions of the self, the official version" (Bollas, 1983, p. 7). Bollas in particular makes the point that a countertransference disclosure has a much better chance of being productive if it is presented as an invitation to "play" with the phenomenon of the therapist's response. By contrast, when the intervention comes across as a complaint, a demand, or an official proclamation, the risk is much higher that the outcome will be disruptive, again because of the likelihood that the patient will experience the therapist as reacting rather than examining.

Similarly, there are occasions when very difficult material for both patient and therapist begins to surface, accompanied by strong interactional pressure and an uncomfortable countertransference response. At such times, a countertransference-based intervention can be very useful if it can be both offered and received as an invitation for an "observational time out." A countertransference-based intervention such as this might be, "I feel as though there is a great deal of tension in the air here that I, for one, do not believe we really understand." Depending on how the patient receives this communication (which is, of course, always the most critical variable), such an intervention can be extremely useful in shifting both participants in the direction of examination and away from what may be developing as a destructive enactment.

Better use can often be made of a therapist's countertransference response when it is used as the basis for a transference intervention or some comment about the interaction rather than as a direct countertransference disclosure. Bollas (1983) refers to this as an intervention "inspired" by the therapist's countertransference response, even though the response itself is not directly made explicit. On the basis of his preparation of the intervention, the therapist may anticipate that a direct countertransference-based intervention such as "I am feeling as though I have to walk on eggshells today with everything I say to you" will be received by the patient as a complaint and a demand for cooperation rather than as an invitation to examine this aspect of the interaction as potentially meaningful. Having made this assessment, the therapist may choose a countertransference-inspired transference interpretation ("You seem pretty fed up with me this morning") or what may appear to be a more neutral observation about the seeming status of the interaction ("We seem to be having a hard time communicating right now"), which, once again, is countertransference inspired in contrast to a direct disclosure. Any of these three uses of the same countransference response may be more or less helpful, depending on the patient, the therapist, and the status of the interaction.

THE IMPACT OF A COUNTERTRANSFERENCE-BASED INTERVENTION

In any consideration of the impact of an intervention, countertransference-based or otherwise, the patient's subjective experience of the therapist is the most important criterion. How the therapist ultimately feels, both about what he has just said and about the patient's response to it, is also important in assessing the impact of an intervention, but it is secondary to the subjective experience of the patient. As Bollas (1983) points out, the therapist should never engage in a countertransference-based intervention for the primary purpose of seeking relief, but he may in fact experience relief as an byproduct of a useful intervention, even though this was not the primary motivating factor. A sense of relief from tension for the patient is often an indication that the particular countertransference-based intervention was well advised. If, however, the patient is shocked by the intervention—and, once again, this applies not only to those interventions which are based on countertransference material—we agree with Bollas that the therapist has demonstrated poor timing and technique, even if the content of the intervention itself was reasonably accurate.

With reference to Winnicott's (1971) concept of potential space, a well-prepared and implemented countertransference-based intervention broadens and enriches the area of "play" between therapist and patient; one that is poorly conceived has precisely the opposite effect of destroying potential space. In the former state of affairs, the patient to some extent is able to accept the invitation to play with the countertransference content that has been offered for mutual and collaborative examination, rather than both parties' experiencing the therapist's response as an actuality that is merely being enacted. The observational posture of both is enhanced. Though the therapist needs to have had sufficient containment-separateness from the induced identification in order to have made a useful intervention, this sense of perspective is still further consolidated by an intervention that has gone well. The patient tends to feel understood, not blamed or criticized. The interaction itself, which may have been headed in the direction of a destructive reenactment of the patient's vicious circle in human relationships, may once again be restored to a balance between observation and experience. Following a useful countertransference-based intervention, valuable connections can be made by both participants between the quality of the current therapeutic interaction and other significant relationships that the patient has experienced.

Finally, it may be that the most useful and significant aspect of a well-prepared and implemented countertransference-based intervention is its role in interrupting the patient's repetitive vicious circle in interpersonal relationships. In the case of the "good enough" therapist who is working well with a patient, the induced identification represents an arousal within the therapist of some aspect of the patient's inner world. As a consequence of the patient's projective identification, the therapist has identified with the patient's internalized self- or object representation, which has been transmitted to the therapist by means of interactional pressure. In the case of a sadomasochistic paradigm, for example, that is being recreated in the therapeutic interaction, a therapist may find himself feeling bullied. In such a situation, the therapist needs to avoid the pitfalls of masochistic submission at the one extreme versus sadistic retaliation at the other. If the therapist is able to "stand up for himself," as Bollas (1983, p. 24) puts it, without becoming harsh or punitive, it is likely that he is also standing up for something in the patient, since the patient has undoubtedly been on the receiving end of what he is currently directing toward the therapist. A countertransference-based intervention is an especially potent way for the therapist to "stand up for himself." An example of such an intervention might be, "I feel as though you believe the only way you can obtain what it is you believe you need from me is through the use of force. I think it is hard for you to believe that two people can have a relationship with one another without someone needing to gain the upper hand." For a more extensive examination of just such a clinical scenario, we refer you to the first of the three vignettes that make up the next chapter.

10 *Clinical Illustrations*

Thus far we have described our schema for processing countertransference reactions with only brief mention of clinical examples. In the present chapter, we shall reverse this emphasis so as to bring more of an experience-near quality to our presentation. We will describe three clinical vignettes in some depth. Each vignette demonstrates various important aspects of countertransference as it is experienced over time in psychoanalytic treament. The vignettes are derived from careful reconstruction of notes of actual case material, with appropriate modifications to protect confidentiality. We have interrupted the flow of the case material at selective points to interject schematic analyses of the manner in which the clinical material depicts aspects of our sequence for processing countertransference reactions.

CASE 1. COUNTERTRANSFERENCE VICTIMIZATION

A successful real estate developer in his late 30s initially sought treatment following the abrupt breakup of a year-long relationship with a woman who lived out of state. The pattern of devastation by abandonment had in fact characterized a number of previous relationships for the patient. This time, however, it was exacerbated by the woman's marrying someone within weeks of the breakup and by the fact that the patient himself had introduced them to one another. In addition, the patient was fearful that he would be unable to sustain his business successes, which required a great deal of time, energy, and creativity. His distress following the breakup was such that his productivity had collapsed. He was well aware of what it was like to struggle financially. He had made a major business breakthrough only shortly before he began to date the girlfriend who ultimately was to leave him. With his newfound success, his income had improved tenfold. But he again found himself deeply concerned that he would be forced to return to a lower middle-class life style after having had "a taste of the good life." The patient had been in psychoanalytic treatment with sliding scale arrangements three times previously for periods of up to three years, always having to terminate prematurely, manifestly because he was no longer able to pay the bills.

In the early months of treatment, it became very clear to both therapist and patient that the relationship with the girlfriend had never been a genuinely close one. The fact that she lived in a distant state limited their contact to a few days each month and to a couple of trips taken together. From the beginning, the patient had believed her to be his inferior, both with respect to intelligence and emotional maturity. He firmly believed that "all she wanted to do was to marry someone rich," and he had consistently indicated to her that he had no such plans in mind. As the examination of the relationship continued, the therapist gathered the impression that the patient had actually viewed the woman with moderate contempt throughout the course of their relationship and that this was not simply a case of retrospective distortion of his feelings following the ultimate rejection. There was considerable evidence pointing to the fact that her "stock had skyrocketed" when she announced that she was breaking off the relationship for another man, at which point the patient became utterly obsessed with her. Although he never once initiated any contact with her from that day forward, he was unable to think of anything else. In the weeks before initiating treatment and for several months thereafter, he suffered from frequent crying spells, nightmares, occasional suicidal thoughts, and an almost total inability to work.

Simultaneously, he continued to enjoy financial success, primarily the result of business deals that had been completed prior to the girlfriend's rejection of him. To compensate for his ongoing psychic pain, he spent his money liberally, always with the anxious feeling that he should be husbanding his resources for what he felt certain were the tough financial times ahead of him. He frequently described waking up in the morning feeling startled by his luxurious surroundings, having to remind himself that this was in fact his own home and thinking that he was undeserving of anything other than the spartan existence he had previously known. The dissonance between his current materialistic and business success on the one hand and his emotional misery on the other became increasingly forceful throughout the first year of treatment.

The patient is the only son of what he described as a depressed, alcoholic mother experienced as engulfing. Father was described as emotionally remote, denigrating the patient's achievements and undermining the patient's autonomy throughout childhood and adulthood. In the patient's experience, father seemed intent on keeping his son at home to take care of his mother so as to keep her "out of his own hair." Although the patient has resisted what he has experienced as the array of bribes and pressures to keep him living in his parents' home, he nevertheless makes frequent trips to the west coast to visit, and he speaks with them on the phone several times a week. He is acutely aware of feelings of bitterness, resentment, and mistrust of his parents—"They make it seem like they are taking care of me when in fact all they are doing is using me for their own purposes. It's always been that way." Finally, the patient appears to have had some form of reportedly life-threatening illness in his first year of life, requiring significant time in the hospital. The details of this are vague in his mind, reflecting what he perceives to be his parents' unwillingness to give details.

With regard to interpersonal relationships in general, the patient believes that there are two types of people in the world —"the quick and the dead," those who are able to gain the upper hand and use it to their own advantage and to the detriment of others, and those who futilely wish they could gain the upper hand. None of his experiences with people has suggested to him that it is possible for two persons to engage in a mutually satisfying relationship in which the needs of both are served, where he with the "upper hand" is neither a saint nor a parasite and he with the "lower hand" is neither a beneficiary of charity nor a victim of exploitation.

His problems in interpersonal relationships came very much to the forefront of the treatment relationship from its inception. Beginning with the initial telephone contact, the patient made it clear that he would be consulting with two other therapists in order to decide with whom he would feel most comfortable. Although the therapist first took this as routine, the issue very quickly seemed to become rich with meaning. Before the patient made his final decision, he and the therapist met a total of four sessions at the patient's request. During this time, the therapist noted in himself a rising sense of anticipation as to whether he would be selected but continued to ascribe this reaction to the overall nature of the situation. In general, he felt that he did not lose perspective by wishing to impress the patient. The therapist enjoyed a successful practice and did not need this patient to keep his hours filled. He did, however, find the patient to be bright, very psychologically minded, well motivated, and able to attend multiple weekly sessions—in short, an excellent candidate for psychoanalytic treatment.

During this evaluation period, the therapist felt very closely scrutinized by the patient. The patient, for his part, seemed to promote in the therapist a feeling of suspense. Even as he made it clear how much he was suffering in his life and how out of control of things he felt in general, in very subtle ways he seemed to take pleasure in having the "upper hand" as to whether or not he would select this therapist. Indeed, this appeared to be the only area of his life in which he did feel in control. At the end of the fourth session, for example, he said very coolly, "Well, as you know, I have to make a decision about whom to see, so I'll have to call you."

THIS MATERIAL SUGGESTS THAT THE PATIENT HAS BEGUN TO ENGAGE IN PROJECTIVE IDENTIFICATION, WHEREBY HE HAS AROUSED WITHIN THE THERAPIST A MODERATE SENSE OF VULNERABILITY TO REJECTION THAT SEEMS TO EXCEED WHAT THE THERAPIST WOULD "ROUTINELY" EXPECT FROM HIMSELF UNDER THESE CIRCUMSTANCES. ALTHOUGH STILL IN ITS INCIPIENT STAGES, THE PATIENT'S INTERACTIONAL PRESSURE APPEARS TO INCLUDE THE OBSERVABLE FEATURES OF EXTENDING THE TIME TO FOUR SESSIONS WHILE REMAINING DECIDEDLY COOL AND NONCOMMITTAL TOWARD THE THERAPIST. THE MANNER IN WHICH THE PATIENT MAY HAVE LED THE THERAPIST TO FEEL CLOSELY SCRUTINIZED HAS NOT BEEN SPECIFIED, BUT THIS MAY ALSO CONTAIN ELEMENTS OF SUBTLE INTERACTIONAL PRESSURE. THE THERAPIST APPEARS TO BE MAINTAINING A REASONABLY BALANCED AND CLEAR MENTAL SET, ALTHOUGH THE APPARENT INTERACTIONAL PRESSURE SEEMS TO BE INDUCING WITHIN HIM AN INCIPIENT IDENTIFICATION OF "PASSIVE-DEPENDENT VICTIM," ACCOMPANIED BY THE SIGNAL AFFECT OF MOUNTING SUSPENSE. WITHIN THE THERAPIST, THE INTROJECTIVE IDENTIFICATION DOES NOT SEEM TO HAVE FULLY CRYSTALLIZED, ALTHOUGH WHAT HE IS EXPERIENCING AT THIS JUNCTURE MAY WELL BE A HARBINGER OF THINGS TO COME. LITTLE IF ANY INTERNAL PROCESSING OF THE INTROJECTIVE IDENTIFICATION BY THE THERAPIST HAS BEEN ALLUDED TO. IT IS NOT YET POSSIBLE FROM THE MATERIAL TO ASSESS EITHER THE THERAPIST'S OWN CONTRIBUTION TO THE INTERACTION OR THE EXTENT OF HIS PERSONAL PROPENSITY TO NEED ACCEPTANCE FROM PATIENTS. A QUESTION MIGHT BE RAISED IN THIS REGARD AS TO WHY HE ALLOWED THE EVALUATION TO EXTEND OVER FOUR SESSIONS, AND WHETHER THIS WAS EXPLORED WITH THE PATIENT.

When in fact the patient did call the therapist soon afterward to say that he would like to work with him, there was a remarkable shift in the patient's tone and presentation. Specifically, he appeared to be anxious and insecure about whether the therapist would be interested in working with him. Apart from commenting on and inquiring about the patient's obvious anxiety, the therapist did not feel he could do much with this interpretively. But he believed that he understood more clearly why he himself had come to feel uncharacteristically nervous about whether he would be selected by the patient.

Looking back over his interaction with the patient, the therapist felt he had been kept in the dark. The evaluation period had been stretched out over several sessions, during which the patient remained manifestly cool about the selection process itself. He never provided any concrete indication of his favorable or unfavorable perception of the therapist and yet delivered many references to the upcoming decision he would have to make. All of this engendered in the therapist a feeling of being "lorded over," a phrase that the patient has subsequently used to describe his experience of relationships. By indicating to the therapist that he would like to work with him, the patient seemed to feel he was surrendering the reins of control to the therapist and opening himself up either for immediate rejection or, worse, for mounting exploitation.

> INTERNAL PROCESSING OF THE PATIENT'S PROJECTIVE IDENTIFICATION HAS CLEARLY BEGUN. THE THERAPIST APPEARS TO BE HANDLING EFFECTIVELY THE TASKS OF CONTAINING THE THOUGHTS, FEELINGS, AND IMPULSES ASSOCIATED WITH THE IDENTIFICATION OF PASSIVE-DEPENDENT VICTIM AS WELL AS SEPARATING SUFFICIENTLY FROM THE IDENTIFICATION SO AS TO BEGIN TO EXAMINE THE MEANINGS OF THE COUNTERTRANSFERENCE RESPONSE. CLEARLY, HOWEVER, HIS EFFORTS TO DO SO SEEM TO HAVE BEEN GREATLY AIDED BY THE PATIENT'S REQUEST TO WORK WITH HIM, THUS TAKING HIM OFF THE "HOT SEAT" OF EVALUATION. THROUGH HIS OBSERVATION OF THE PATIENT'S SUBSEQUENT ANXIETY THAT THE THERAPIST MIGHT NOW BE UNWILLING TO ACCEPT HIM, THE THERAPIST RECOGNIZED THE APPARENT ROLE REVERSAL. BY UTILIZING THE PATIENT-INTERACTION WORKING MODEL AND THE THERAPIST-INTERACTION WORKING MODEL, THE THERAPIST HAS HYPOTHESIZED THAT THE PATIENT HAS SUCCESSFULLY INDUCED WITHIN HIM A TASTE OF WHAT IT FEELS LIKE TO BE FEARING REJECTION HELPLESSLY. ALTHOUGH THE THERAPIST HAS NOT SPELLED THIS OUT, HE APPEARS TO FEEL THAT THE PATIENT HAS UNCONSCIOUSLY ORCHESTRATED THIS ROLE REVERSAL AS A DEFENSE AGAINST HIS OWN FEAR OF REJECTION BY THE THERAPIST. GIVEN THE PRESENTING PROBLEM THAT

BROUGHT THE PATIENT INTO TREATMENT, IT MAY ALSO BE AN UNCONSCIOUS COMMUNICATION VIA PROJECTIVE IDENTIFICATION OF HIS CORE DIFFICULTIES IN INTERPERSONAL RELATIONSHIPS. IN A PRELIMINARY FASHION, LACKING IN SUBSTANTIAL VALIDATION, THE THERAPIST APPEARS TO HAVE MADE SOME MOVEMENT SCHEMATICALLY INTO THE EMPATHIC CONNECTION SUBPHASE OF INTERNAL PROCESSING, ALTHOUGH NO EXPLICIT COMMUNICATION HAS YET OCCURRED.

At this very early stage of the treatment, the therapist could not fully appreciate how central and compelling an issue this would be for the therapeutic relationship. In the first several months of treatment, the patient's depressive crisis over the rejection by his former girlfriend continued unabated. Though his misery seemed quite genuine, some headway was able to be made in illuminating what seemed to be the patient's unconscious need to fail miserably in a relationship so as to assuage his intense feelings of unconscious guilt over having become suddenly and tremendously successful in his business pursuits. From his previous analytic work, the patient needed no introduction to unconscious processes. The therapist experienced a strong sense of useful collaboration with the patient in the investigation of the hypothesis about the patient's need to suffer so as to compensate for feelings of undeserved pleasure and success. This need was linked genetically with what appeared to be an unconscious, Faustian compromise with his parents, namely, "I will leave you. I will not live out my years in your home caring for my mother and failing in life so as to protect my father's sense of adequacy. But in order that you will not hate me and refuse to allow me ever to return, I will obey your wish that I live an unhappy life of failure, especially in intimate relationships."

Invariably during sessions in which this material was being explored, the momentary experience of useful collaboration would give way within the patient to feelings of agitation, upheaval, and despair. From feelings of sad but useful insight and seeming appreciation for the therapist's help, the transition into a violent upsurge of despair and criticism of the therapist was frequently begun with comments such as, "You know, in this sort of therapy, no matter how bad you think it is, it's always worse. The more bad things you find out about yourself, the more bad things there are always left to find." Typically, the remainder of such a session was characterized by an outpouring of hopelessness, futility, and despair. Subsequent sessions would be dominated by bitter attacks against the therapist's competence and honesty, with frequent allusions to breaking off the treatment in order to find a therapist "who won't hurt me."

As the treatment unfolded over the first several months, the therapist's countertransference response to the patient became a study in contrasts. On one hand, the therapist found the patient to be likeable, engaging, and exceptionally interesting, much of the time. Despite the frequent verbal assaults, the therapist often looked forward to the sessions, which he usually found to be challenging and stimulating. On the other hand, there were times when the therapist was aware of feeling defensive, indignant, and a sense of "who needs this."

> THE PATIENT'S "ATTACKS ON THE THERAPIST'S HONESTY AND COMPETENCE," AS WELL AS HIS REFERENCES TO THE THERAPIST'S HURTING HIM, APPEAR TO REPRESENT AN ESCALATION OF INTERACTIONAL PRESSURE, EFFECTIVELY CASTING THE THERAPIST IN THE ROLE OF ONE WHO EXPLOITS A HELPLESS VICTIM. EXPERIENTIALLY, HOWEVER, THE THERAPIST HIMSELF OCCUPIES THE ROLE OF VICTIM AS THE TARGET OF THE PATIENT'S COMPLAINTS AND INSINUATIONS. THE THERAPIST'S DEFENSIVE AND INDIGNANT FEELINGS APPEAR TO REPRESENT SIGNAL AFFECTS, SUGGESTING THAT HIS INTROJECTIVE IDENTIFICATION IS INDEED FALLING ON THE SIDE OF VICTIM RATHER THAN VICTIMIZER. THAT THE THERAPIST CONTINUES TO MAINTAIN A POSITIVE VIEW OF THE PATIENT IN THE FACE OF HIS DEROGATORY INTERACTIONAL PRESSURE INDICATES THAT THE PATIENT'S PROJECTIVE IDENTIFICATION HAS NOT YET BECOME DISRUPTIVE TO THE TREATMENT. THERE IS NO EXPLICIT EVIDENCE OF FURTHER INTERNAL PROCESSING BEYOND WHAT WE MAY CONSIDER TO BE THE THERAPIST'S ONGOING CONTAINMENT OF THE FEELINGS AND IMPULSES ASSOCIATED WITH THE EXPERIENCE OF VICTIMIZATION.

In what seemed to be a paradoxical effect, the patient's insight into the unconsciously active role he may have played in his failed relationship seemed to be accompanied by an exacerbation of depressive symptomatology (nightmares, crying spells, inability to concentrate, suicidal thoughts). The patient and, to a lesser degree, the therapist experienced a mounting sense of frustration and concern as the months passed. Efforts at examining the here-and-now issues within the transference never seemed to get off the ground in any meaningful way. In one noteworthy session, nearly a full year into twice weekly treatment, the patient immediately opened with the following salvo:

> P: You know, if I had known that coming here was going to make me worse, I never would have done this. I've been coming here for eleven months and I've never been in more agony in my life. My friends go to their therapists and actually get better. They all think I'm nuts for continuing to come to you. They all think you can't possibly know what the hell you are doing. I keep pouring thousands and thousands of dollars into this because I feel I have nowhere else to turn, and you just keep making me worse. You should have told me this was going to happen before we started and I would have just written you the check. That way, you would have gotten what you are after and at least I wouldn't be tortured like this.

The patient continued in this vein for several minutes. In response to the therapist's question as to how, specifically, he was torturing the patient, the patient was able to say nothing beyond vague comments about the process (e.g., "No matter how bad you think it is, you always find out it's worse"). As this tirade washed over him, the therapist made a concerted effort to take note of his own experience with the patient. Despite the fortification of having weathered many such barrages previously from this patient, the therapist's immediate sinking feeling was essentially, "Damn it, here we go again," followed by mounting anger, indignation, and an impulse to retaliate. The therapist fantasized saying to the patient, "Fine, you pathetic son-of-a-bitch, if that's how you feel, there's the door!" As the patient's verbal assault continued, such feelings in the therapist alternated with a sense of submission that, in fact, the patient's accusations were entirely warranted and that he himself deserved to be pummeled in this fashion.

> THERE ARE CLEAR INDICATIONS THAT THE PATIENT'S ESCALATING INTERACTIONAL PRESSURE IS HITTING HOME. INCREASINGLY, THE ALTERNATING SIGNAL AFFECT OF

SINKING SUBMISSION IN COUNTERPOINT TO RETALIATORY ANGER AND INDIGNATION STRONGLY SUGGESTS THAT THE THERAPIST IS OSCILLATING BETWEEN POLAR INTROJECTIVE IDENTIFICATIONS. ON ONE HAND, HE IS EXPERIENCING A VICTIMIZED TRIAL IDENTIFICATION WITH THE PATIENT AS HIS ASSAULTING OBJECT; ON THE OTHER HAND, HE EXPERIENCES AN IMPULSE TO TURN THE TABLES AND ASSUME THE ASSAULTING ROLE. THIS APPEARS TO BE A CRITICAL MOMENT IN TREATMENT, GIVEN THE IMPULSES AND FEELINGS THAT THE THERAPIST IS STRUGGLING TO CONTAIN.

Having been through this before with the patient, though never with so high a level of intensity, the therapist struggled to remind himself that they had always survived similar experiences before without disaster occurring. By drawing on those memories, the therapist was able to take heart and gather himself in an effort to pull back from the induced, alternating trial identifications. As the patient continued in his attack, the therapist shifted his listening perspective to obtain a better idea of the patient's subjective viewpoint. In so doing, he actively imagined himself as the patient attacking the therapist at this particular point in the treatment. The therapist-as-patient suddenly realized that his attack against the therapist was not altogether as vigorous and convincing as it might have been if his verbal communication were in fact the whole story. He remembered that this issue had come up on previous occasions and that he himself had told the therapist that he realized he was "voting with his feet and with his checkbook" on behalf of the value of the treatment. With this memory at the forefront, the therapist-as-patient became aware of an element of fear of the therapist, who had actually become very important to him, rendering him vulnerable to the gross exploitation and victimization he had come to expect in all such intimate situations.

THIS MATERIAL ILLUSTRATES WHAT APPEARS TO BE A SUCCESSFUL CONTAINMENT BY THE THERAPIST OF THE POTENT IMPULSES AND FEELINGS ASSOCIATED WITH THE INDUCED, ALTERNATING TRIAL IDENTIFICATIONS, BOTH VICTIM AND VICTIMIZING IN NATURE. THE WORK OF THE CONTAINMENT-SEPARATENESS SUBPHASE PROVIDES THE FOUNDATION FOR THE UTILIZATION OF THE WORKING

> MODELS. SINCE THE THERAPIST ALREADY HAS A FAIRLY CLEAR PICTURE OF HIS OWN UNCOMFORTABLE SENSE OF SELF—BOTH AS VICTIM AND VICTIMIZER—HE UTILIZES THE PATIENT-INTERACTION WORKING MODEL IN AN EFFORT TO UNDERSTAND MORE ABOUT THE EMOTIONAL EXPERIENCE OF THE PATIENT IN THE CURRENT INTERACTION. BY IMAGINING HIMSELF AS THE PATIENT, HE IS ABLE TO ILLUMINATE THE HIDDEN SENSE OF FEAR THAT THE PATIENT MAY BE EXPERIENCING. IT CAN ALSO BE INFERRED THAT THE THERAPIST'S UTILIZATION OF THE PATIENT-INTERACTION WORKING MODEL SERVES TO ENHANCE THE THERAPIST'S CONTAINMENT-SEPARATENESS FUNCTIONS, THUS ILLUSTRATING THE MUTUAL INTERPLAY OF THESE TWO SUBPHASES. ALTHOUGH IT IS NOT EXPLICITLY STATED THAT THE THERAPIST FEELS CALMER AND MORE IN CONTROL, THIS SEEMS EVIDENT FROM HIS ABILITY TO ADVANCE THE FORTHCOMING INTERPRETATIONS. THERE CONTINUES TO BE AN ABSENCE OF REFERENCES TO AN EXAMINATION OF THE THERAPIST'S OWN PROPENSITIES AS THEY MAY BE CONTRIBUTING TO THE CURRENT INTERACTION, A GAP IN VALIDATION THAT WOULD BE USEFULLY RECTIFIED.

The therapist-as-patient then actively imagined how he might respond to a variety of different interventions aimed at illuminating his defensive assaultiveness. Memories of past explorations by the therapist and patient centering on the issue of the patient's angry attacks came to mind in which the patient had been directly able to address his own and the therapist's experience. In response to his silent recollections, the therapist offered the following comment:

> T: At the risk of appearing to minimize your complaints, as you know, I believe that your coming here has become very important to you. When you act like this, I believe you are, at the back of your mind, testing me for my response, and that it would not surprise you one bit if I were to say to you something like, "Fine, if that's how you feel, there's the door." (At this point, the therapist noticed that the patient, who had become totally silent, sighed deeply. The therapist quickly assessed that the patient was receptive to what had been said and decided to continue further with his line of interpretation.) On one hand, if I were to say this to you, I believe that this would lead you to feel very

relieved since the feeling of reliance upon me that is developing for you in here makes you feel wide open to bad treatment from me. Since you expect something like that to happen sooner or later, at least that would get it over with and end the awful feeling of suspense I believe you are enduring. On the other hand, I can't help but believe that if I were to say something like that to you, you would also feel very sad indeed. It would confirm to you not only my own unreliability, but also what you believe to be your own innate badness and ability to drive people away. You wouldn't know who to blame more—you or me.

> This is the first direct reference to an explicit, verbal communication dealing with the countertransference material. Since it contains elements derived from the therapist's assessment both of his own countertransference experience as well as the patient's transference experience, the intervention is schematically categorized as a transference/countertransference-based communication. Although the therapist leaves open the question of whether or not he actually had felt the impulse to tell the patient to leave, the fact that the experience is directly alluded to illustrates what Bollas (1983) refers to as a direct use of countertransference disclosure. From the point of view of validation of his hypothesis that his countertransference experience is in fact heavily influenced by the patient's projective identification, the therapist appears to have noted three converging lines of inference: clearly observable interactional pressure from the patient, a clear complementary correspondence between the experiences of patient and therapist, and the paradigmatic nature for the patient of the victim-victimizer relationship. The therapist is also advancing his hypothesis that the current scenario has a particular meaning based upon a repetition of past trauma in relationships.

In the latter stage of this interpretation, the therapist observed the patient subtly nodding his head; this observation was in part responsible for the length of the interpretation. After this intervention, there was a pause of nearly a minute, broken by the following interchange:

P: I think there may be something to what you are saying. This isn't easy for me to say, but I do enjoy the attention I get here. But my life is still just so miserable that I really am afraid that you will use all of that against me and hurt me in some way.

T: Any idea how I would hurt you?

P: (sadly) I don't really know, but I could see 5 or 10 years from now still feeling this bad, maybe my money would even run out, and you'd toss me aside like so much trash.

THIS MATERIAL PROVIDES POSTINTERPRETIVE VALIDATION OF THE THERAPIST'S HYPOTHESES AS TO THE SOURCE AND MEANING OF THE ORIGINAL COUNTERTRANSFERENCE RESPONSE. THE EXPLICIT AGREEMENT FROM THE PATIENT IS CONSISTENT WITH THE SHIFT TO WHAT APPEARS TO BE AN ATMOSPHERE OF GREATER COMFORT AND ENHANCED COMMUNICATION.

During this exchange and the brief silence that ensued, the therapist focused his attention once more on the patient's subjective viewpoint. As the subject of time was mentioned, it suddenly occurred to the therapist that perhaps the vehemence with which the patient's attack had been launched was in part fueled by the one-year anniversary of the treatment that was fast approaching.

T: Any idea why all of this is coming up so forcefully right now?

P: No, not really. Do you?

T: Well, when you referred to the years rolling by and not getting any help as one of the things that really scares you, I suddenly realized that we have the one year anniversary of the treatment coming up. As we've discussed, crossing over that point in time really does worry you because it makes you think that, *then*, I'll *really* know how much you rely upon me and I'll *really* have you under my bootheel.

P: (pause) You could be right. (pause, sadly) I feel defeated. I told myself that unless I really felt as though I was getting help that I would stop at the one year point. Now I've got no one to blame but myself.

T: You mean you can't blame me if I really do hurt you?

P: Well, I can blame you, but it's really me that's asking for it. I've never known anything else, so why should this be any different. But here I go again, opening myself up for abuse and feeling like I just can't stop myself. I'm disgusted with myself, all for a little attention, because I'm desperate and don't know who else to turn to. Why should anybody else be any different?

The therapist felt that the patient's response tended to validate that his line of interpretation was in a useful direction. Though the issues involved were in no way resolved, a potentially destructive reenactment of attack and counterattack was averted. In addition, greater access to some of the underlying issues had been gained. For the remainder of this session, given that the patient's defensive assault on the therapist had shifted to self-disgust, the therapist was able to engage the patient in an examination of why the patient's fears, wishes, and beliefs were what they were.

THE THERAPIST HAS FORMULATED AN ADDITIONAL HYPOTHESIS AS TO A POTENTIAL MEANING OF THE PATIENT'S THOUGHTS, FEELINGS, AND ACTION. THE RESPONSE APPEARS CONFIRMATORY THAT THE PATIENT'S MODE OF INTERACTION REPRESENTS NOT ONLY A RE-CREATION OF PAST TRAUMA WITHIN THE CURRENT INTERACTION, BUT ALSO AN UNCONSCIOUS ATTEMPT TO STRUGGLE WITH A PARTICULAR ADAPTIVE CONTEXT IN THE TREATMENT; NAMELY, THE ONE-YEAR ANNIVERSARY OF BEGINNING TREATMENT. THIS APPEARS TO HAVE THE SPECIAL MEANING FOR THE PATIENT OF AROUSING SELF-DISGUST AND A DESPERATE SENSE OF BEING UNABLE TO PROTECT HIMSELF FROM WHAT HE FEARS WILL LEAD TO INEVITABLE VICTIMIZATION.

A few months later, the therapist once again found himself caught in a similar countertransference dilemma, in which he felt the pull of submission alternating with an impulse toward defensive retaliation. The patient began one session by describing a recent phone conversation with his father. The patient had just appeared in a television interview dealing with his area of professional expertise. In a very deflated tone, he offered the following:

P: Here I am being interviewed on TV because I'm supposed to know something about something. All my friends who saw the program had nothing but good things to say about how I did. So my father calls me on the phone, all he can say about me is that he thought I should have sat up straighter and I should have unbuttoned my jacket. No praise, not one positive word to say. The son-of-a-bitch is so threatened by the fact that I'm doing well that he has to find something to pick on. He doesn't know a damn thing about my work so he tells me my jacket should have been unbuttoned. No wonder I don't feel I deserve that life should go well for me.

T: How did you respond to your father?

P: Respond! I didn't say anything. In the first place, he was just behaving the way he always has. What was I going to do, scream at him? That would just make matters worse. He's got a hell of a temper, and I know he's never going to change. So what would be the point? No, I just sat there and took it until I could figure out a way to get off the phone.

At this point, the therapist observed that he understood how upsetting the conversation must have been for the patient. After a brief silence, the therapist stated that perhaps the patient was similarly upset with him either because he had not seen the program or, if he had, like father, he was offering no praise. This effort went nowhere, leading the therapist to believe that this was in fact not an issue.

For the next several minutes, the material seemed to have no direction. There were long silences interspersed with ruminations by the patient as to how bad things were going in life and how hopeless he felt. The therapist recognized in advance that the patient was heading toward a complaint about the inefficacy of the treatment, the patient's feelings of disgust with himself for becoming "addicted" to a treatment that only made him worse, and the like. Indeed, hardly a session went by without at least some minor reference to his dissatisfaction with the treatment. But the therapist did not anticipate the escalating vehemence and causticity of the patient's attack, even though he had come to know very well the patient's propensity in this direction.

As anticipated, the patient began impugning the therapist's competence, integrity, and intention, insisting that the entire treatment was a travesty serving only to disguise the therapist's avarice. The therapist had been through similar diatribes before with this patient. Yet there was something about the viciousness and intensity of this particular attack that caused the therapist's blood to begin to boil. Taking this as a signal affect, he attempted to pay a great deal of attention to what he himself was thinking and experiencing as the patient's attack continued to unfold. He became aware of a sense of rising indignation, a feeling of, "After all I've done, after all my hard work, I simply do not deserve to be attacked in this way." As in the past, this sense of things was associated with an impulse to strike back at the patient. But as he paid closer and closer attention to his own experience of the patient's attack, the therapist also discovered in himself a feeling of hopelessness and inadequacy concerning his ability ever to help this patient in any enduring way. This aspect of his experience with the patient seemed to support the patient's accusations and left him with a feeling of hopeless resignation that perhaps in some secret way the patient was "right" after all. Thus, the therapist was aware of an eagerness for the session to end so that the emotional beating could be over.

> THE THERAPIST, ONCE AGAIN, APPEARS TO BE RESPONDING TO INTENSE INTERACTIONAL PRESSURE FROM THE PATIENT WITH ALTERNATING TRIAL IDENTIFICATIONS, RETALIATORY SHIFTING TO SUBMISSIVE. THE THERAPIST APPEARS TO BE MAKING HEAVY USE OF THE THERAPIST-INTERACTION WORKING MODEL TO MONITOR THE ACCOMPANYING SIGNAL AFFECTS AS CLOSELY AS POSSIBLE.

Suddenly, the wish to extricate himself from the patient reminded the therapist of the patient's attitude toward the phone call with his father—"I just sat there and took it until I could figure out a way ot get off the phone." At this juncture, the therapist felt a rush of understanding of the immediate underlying meaning of the patient's tirade, recalling the salient points about the conversation with father—feelings of anger and outrage, the expression of which would only make matters worse; a sense of futility and despair, accompanied by hopeless submission until such time as a retreat could be effected. All these points corresponded to elements of the therapist's reaction to the patient's attack.

> UTILIZATION OF THE THERAPIST-INTERACTION WORKING MODEL APPEARS TO HAVE LED TO WHAT MAY BE A CRITICAL INSIGHT FOR THE THERAPIST. ALTHOUGH THE

> CURRENT INTERACTION BETWEEN PATIENT AND THERAPIST INVOLVES COMPLEMENTARY IDENTIFICATIONS, THE STRONG POSSIBILITY EXISTS THAT THE THERAPIST'S IDENTIFICATORY EXPERIENCE AT THE HANDS OF THE PATIENT IS ACTUALLY CONCORDANT WITH WHAT THE PATIENT HAS JUST DESCRIBED AT THE HANDS OF HIS FATHER

With this insight in mind, the therapist shifted his primary attention to the patient's experience of the interaction. The verbal assault was still raging. The therapist now began to feel excited about the understanding of the patient that was suddenly coming together, even though it was still incomplete and not fully confirmed. Clearly, despite the patient's continuing attack, the therapist himself no longer felt either the impulse to counterattack or the sense that he deserved to suffer. This placed him in an excellent position to examine the patient's immediate experience since his own house was now in much better order.

> ALTHOUGH NOT BY ITSELF SUFFICIENTLY VALIDATING OF THE UNDERLYING HYPOTHESIS, THE THERAPIST'S RENEWED SENSE OF PERSPECTIVE DOES LEND SUPPORT AND EVINCES INCREASING SUCCESS IN THE TASKS OF THE CONTAINMENT-SEPARATENESS SUBPHASE.

By actively imagining himself to be the patient, the therapist-as-patient realized first hand several distinct aspects of the patient's experience. First, there was a feeling of being criticized by the therapist for not handling the situation with his father more forcefully. Second, the patient seemed unconsciously to be conveying to the therapist, "If you're so clever and you think you can handle that kind of devastating attack any better, I'll have to see it with my own eyes." Third, there was a desperation behind the patient's words that implied "I need your help—please show me that there is some way to have a relationship without having to be either abusive or abused." Finally, the therapist-as-patient realized that concealed beneath the patient's surface viciousness was a deep fear that the therapist would in fact let him down and either retaliate or submit, either of which would confirm his conviction that this was the way of all human relationships.

THE THERAPIST'S IMMERSION IN THE LISTENING PERSPECTIVE OF THE PATIENT-INTERACTION WORKING MODEL APPEARS TO HAVE GENERATED SEVERAL HYPOTHESES AS TO THE UNDERLYING MEANINGS OF THE CURRENT INTERACTION. ALTHOUGH EACH APPEARS PLAUSIBLE, FURTHER EFFORTS AT VALIDATION ARE CALLED FOR.

At this point, the therapist felt very strongly that some intervention was called for; to say nothing would clearly be construed by the patient as a submissive confirmation of the accusations he was leveling. At the same time, the therapist believed that the patient feared and partly expected a forceful counterattack, although at this juncture of the therapist's processing of the material, he realized that this was no longer a concern since he now had a firm grip on his own emotional state. The therapist felt that in some way he needed to stand up for himself (see Bollas, 1983) because in so doing he would also be standing up for some aspect of the patient, now located within himself, that the patient himself had great difficulty standing up for. Weighing all these possibilities, he made the following interpretation in a firm but gentle voice during a lull in the patient's abuse:

T: I admit that what I am about to say feels a little risky to me, but given all that you've said, I feel as though saying nothing would be worse. Among all of your complaints and accusations, you've said that you are worse off now than when you came here. I respect the fact that you feel that way at the moment, but I have to say that I do not think that squares with how I believe you are now compared to the shape you were in when you first came. In part, my hesitance in talking about this is because it makes me feel a little like a used car salesman, which is personally distasteful. But whether or not these changes are attributable to therapy or the passage of time, or for that matter the alignment of celestial bodies, in my opinion, you are nowhere near as depressed as when you came in. You no longer have crying spells, nightmares, or suicidal thoughts. You're able to concentrate on your work, and have once again become very productive. I also think you are feeling better about yourself, you're less isolated, and our alliance—believe it or not—seems to me to be much more solid. But those things are far more open to opinion, so let's try to stick with the more "objective" measures of improvement.

P: Oh, I see, and you want all the credit for that.

T: Well, I understand why you could see me trying to take credit, and perhaps you're right. But my intention is to try to understand what's making you so tremendously upset right now.

P: Then why don't you try listening to me for a change.

T: In my own way, however inept it may seem to you, that is precisely what I have been trying to do. (quietly and gently) But is that all you really want me to do, just shut up and listen?

P: (silence)

T: I believe what you are feeling is more important than anything else. What concerns me is that we won't ever be able to get to the bottom of your feelings if we pay attention only to what you are saying.

P: Fine. So what's your latest brilliant idea?

T: In some way, I believe that what has taken place between you and me over the last several minutes is reminiscent of the conversation you had with your father.

P: (quietly, after a pause of several seconds) How do you mean?

T: Well, I'm not sure, but it feels to me as though I am now in the same position with you that you felt you were in with your father. Only now, the shoe is on the other foot for you.

P: (silence) I see your point. (pause) Could be. (pause) But I still don't see what you're driving at.

T: As I was listening to your comments, at first I felt as though I had only two options, which were probably the same two options that, in general, you felt you had with respect to your father—either fight fire with fire, respond in kind, and really have a big fight, or just sit there and take it, say nothing, and wait for the abuse to be over. It took me awhile to realize that there was yet a third option. I realized that I could at least try to stand up for myself without feeling as though I was just trying to get even, and I realized that I could do that, not by arguing with you, but by trying to understand some of the deeper meanings of what has been happening here today.

P: (long silence). But my father will never change so what's the point?

T: Your father may never change. But I think the point has more to do with finding some way to stick up for yourself, because I think you pay a high price when you take everything he says very much to heart.

P: And so you think I just came in here looking for somebody to dump on since I got dumped on.

T: Not really. You may never have had to attack me in the way you did if you felt as though I really understood your problem with your father when we first talked about it. I think there is a good chance you did not feel that I was really with you when I questioned your response to your father's criticism. Whether or not you intended to accomplish this—either consciously or unconsciously—the outcome of your actions was such that you placed me in a position where I would at least have the opportunity to understand what it was like to get that kind of criticism from your father. It is as though you gave me the opportunity to experience that, in my own way, firsthand.

P: (long pause) I felt like you thought I should have been able to confront my father, and that I was some kind of wimp for not blasting him back. When I get screwed over, I know that I tend to turn around and do the same thing to other people. (long pause) But you don't sound mad.

Once again, although the underlying issues are in no way resolved, a repetition of a vicious circle has been averted. The therapist has presented the patient with a different way of handling a situation that has always been very difficult for him. This exchange contains elements of a new experience for the patient, made possible by the development of insight, first within the therapist, then conveyed to and incorporated by the patient.

THE THERAPIST HAS MADE A TRANSFERENCE/COUNTERTRANSFERENCE-BASED INTERPRETATION TO THE PATIENT. HE IS BASING HIS FORMULATION ON THE CLOSE PARALLELS—ALBEIT WITH ROLE REVERSAL—BETWEEN THE CURRENT EXPERIENCES OF HIMSELF AND HIS PATIENT ON THE ONE HAND WITH THE INTERACTION JUST REPORTED BETWEEN PATIENT AND FATHER, ON THE OTHER. THE WORKING HYPOTHESIS AS TO THE UNDERLYING MEANING OF THE CURRENT INTERACTION RECEIVES VALIDATING SUPPORT FROM THE APPARENT CLOSENESS OF THIS PARALLEL; FROM THE IDENTIFIABLE ADAPTIVE CONTEXT TO WHICH THE PATIENT APPEARS TO BE RESPONDING—NAMELY, THE THERAPIST HAVING BEEN EXPERIENCED AS CRITICAL; FROM THE OBVIOUS COMMUNICATIVE POTENCY OF THE CURRENT INTERACTION; FROM THE THERAPIST'S SENSE OF GREATER CALM, CONTROL, AND EVEN ENTHUSIASM PRIOR TO THE INTERVENTION; AND LASTLY FROM THE PATIENT'S POSITIVE RESPONSE TO THE INTERVENTION, BOTH EXPLICITLY AND BEHAVIORALLY CONFIRMING THE USEFULNESS OF THE THERAPIST'S FORMULATION. THE

ABSENCE OF NONCOMFIRMATORY EVIDENCE IN CONJUNCTION WITH THE VALIDATING CONVERGENCE OF SEVERAL LINES OF INFERENCE DELIVER PERSUASIVE SUPPORT FOR THE THERAPIST'S CONSTRUCTIVE UTILIZATION OF A POTENTIALLY DESTRUCTIVE COUNTERTRANSFERENCE STATE.

CASE 2. COUNTERTRANSFERENCE CONTEMPT AND GUILT

The patient is a woman in her late 30s who has been in treatment for seven years. She began treatment three times per week, but for the last several years has been coming five times a week. The physical arrangement is characterized by a variety of "nesting behaviors" on the patient's part. Although she faces the therapist, she reclines in her chair and makes use of a footrest. She surrounds herself with two pillows taken from the therapist's couch, as well as two medium-sized blankets of her own. In addition, the patient has requested that the blinds be closed on the two large windows that are in her immediate visual field, allowing for a greater consistency of the physical space regardless of time of day or weather conditions.

The patient initially came for treatment as she neared completion of a master's degree in business from a prestigious university. Despite a fine academic record, she had begun to encounter mounting difficulty with job interviews, which resulted in repeated rejections. Having no real friends and few acquaintances, she was exceedingly anxious about giving up the role of student, which had allowed her contact with people but without the burden of intimacy.

The patient is of Asian extraction, born to a very wealthy family living in a small Far Eastern country. At 16, she came to America to complete her high school education. After graduating from college, she elected to remain in the States and for the next several years worked at a variety of jobs while completing master's degrees in mathematics and computer science. During this time she had to support herself and resist pressure from the family to return to Asia. A few years before the patient began treatment, her mother died, and she experienced mounting pressure to return home to live with her father so that he would not be alone. The patient resented this pressure enormously since she felt that her family not only had not supported her throughout her life, but in fact had actively sabotaged her growth and development.

The patient has a brother 1½ years older than she as well as a younger sister and brother. The care of the children was relegated to a variety of servants and governesses. The mother was described as having been extremely hot tempered and self-absorbed, such that even the servants could not tolerate her abusiveness, leading to a high turnover rate with the accompanying inconsistencies in childcare. Father was experienced as essentially absent and seldom seen, either engrossed with his businesses or remaining in the separate wing of the house in which both parents spent most of their time.

When the patient was approximately two years old, her mother reportedly went to a nearby country with the older brother, who had a serious illness requiring more advanced medical care than was available locally. The mother and brother did not return for nearly two years. The details of this event are hazy, but from what the patient has been able to piece together, she believes that there may well have been trouble in the marriage, prolonging the absence beyond what was medically necessary. Prior to the mother's departure, the patient had apparently begun to talk and use words at an age-appropriate level. But she had been told that she did not speak at all during the entire time that mother was away. The patient understands that upon mother's return, mother had an immediate blowup with the servant who had been primarily responsible for the patient's care; the servant was abruptly fired. The patient was reportedly nearly five before she actively resumed the use of words in speech. Both Chinese and English were spoken by the family and taught in the schools. The patient believes that she has always had major difficulty with each language in both written and spoken forms.

The patient has many memories that she believes supports her conclusion that her mother consciously despised her and wished her harm. As an example, the patient states that when she was an adolescent her weight fluctuated wildly as a consequence of what has since been diagnosed as a thyroid condition. Despite the fact that there was a repeated history of this disorder in the family and the symptoms might well have been recognized, the patient's condition was not treated until she herself sought treatment as an adult.

At the outset of psychotherapy, the level of the patient's emotional difficulties became apparent very quickly. The therapist learned that in stark contrast to the patient's high level of functioning with regard to her academic and professional life, the patient was emotionally very attached to a collection of stuffed animals. Though she had a handful of acquaintances, her strongest attachments were to these inanimate objects. In the privacy of her apartment, she constantly carried on conversations and engaged in play activity with them, each of which was imbued with a distinct personality and given a special name, as one might expect from a three or four year old.

It was also very clear that this woman believed very much in the existence of ghosts and spirits and, in particular, felt convinced that her mother, though dead for several years, continued to haunt and sabotage her in a variety of ways. When things seemed to be going well in the treatment, the patient became especially wary that her mother would be displeased and looking for opportunities to undermine her efforts. At such times, if a random sound or knock drifted into the office from an adjoining suite during a session, or if the therapist's answering maching clicked on indicating a call, the patient would often look at him in obvious fear and ask, "My mother?" Although the patient was highly vulnerable to strained reality testing and given to persecutory thoughts, the therapist did not consider her to be schizophrenic.

For the first several years of treatment, very good progress was made. Almost immediately, the patient became profoundly attached to and reliant on the therapist. The extreme dependency did not trouble the therapist, especially since the patient was almost always able to manage herself between sessions. He found the patient to be extremely bright, witty, likeable, and well able to make use of interpretations, which appeared to have real impact on her level of psychological organization and the quality of her life. At the same time, the depths of her emotional difficulties made her, for the therapist, a fascinating person to know and work with. With all the ups and downs of the treatment, an atmosphere of mutual fondness developed.

Although it is impossible to summarize the treatment in anything but a cursory fashion, there is no question that the patient has made dramatic improvement. For example, she has long understood that her fear of her mother's persecutory spirit does not come from the external presence of an actual ghost, but from her own internalized object representation of her mother, accompanied by the imprint of what the patient experienced as the mother's hateful wishes. She understands that her fear comes from inside, not outside. That this represents a solid insight that the patient has incorporated is attested to by the fact that even under circumstances of extreme stress, although she may have nightmares of ominous female figures, for years she has not mentioned a sense that her mother's spirit was near. Rather, the therapist and patient speak of the patient's own unconscious efforts to get in her own way so as to remain a loyal daughter and so as not to have to face the guilt associated with what she experiences as undeserved and enviable success.

Similarly, the patient has become much more involved with people, albeit still very much at arm's length, with a concomitant diminution in her attachments to her stuffed animals. There was a very definite point in the treatment at which the patient became extremely upset with the therapist because her interactions with her inanimate "circle of friends" had all but lost their heretofore soothing and comforting characteristics. This alarmed the patient because, although she recognized it as her own growing humanization, she felt very afraid that if she "ever needed to go back to my colleagues" she would no longer be able to do so because their soothing properties had faded. Both therapist and patient were fully aware that the patient had transferred her dependency needs entirely into the relationship with the therapist. For several months, she experienced an unmistakable mourning period for the loss of her "associates," which would never again be the same for her.

In approximately the sixth year of treatment, the therapist became increasingly aware that he had begun to feel easily annoyed and irritated by the patient's eccentricities. Previously, there had been only intermittent episodes of this kind of countertransference response. One such episode had been provoked when the patient, on arriving for a session, had obliviously left a trail of muddy footprints on the freshly cleaned carpet.

From such experiences as this, the therapist had had a taste of the mother's apparent wish for her not to exist. But experiences earlier in the treatment represented only a prelude to the more ongoing countertransference attitude that subsequently developed.

The countertransference attitude with which the therapist increasingly came to struggle comprised a variety of characteristics. Whereas previously the therapist's attitude toward the patient had been predominantly one of tolerance, interest, and indeed fondness, these qualities were increasingly eroded by their opposites. With some guilt and alarm, the therapist noted his easily aroused annoyance with the patient's wide variety of peculiar behavior and had to restrain himself from hostile comment. He was all too aware of the patient's profoundly dependent attachment and of his own growing intolerance of what had come to feel like the patient's clinging. He found himself, for example, resenting that the patient monopolized session times that could have been offered to other patients, and he began to be plagued by a feeling that he was spending more one-on-one, undistracted time with this patient than with the individual members of his own family. In general, his experience with the patient came to resemble that of the mother of a six month old who feels worn down by symbiotic exhaustion and the accompanying sense of entrapment.

Examining the sources of his countertransference difficulties, the therapist concluded that the patient's massive speech and language problems were the most obvious and glaring factors. The patient's style of communicating included extremely rapid speech, tremendously minute and irrelevant detail, abrupt shifts—often in mid-sentence—from one subject to another, very poor syntax, repeated misuse of words and phrases, and, most important, profound difficulties with pronunciation. Under circumstances of stress, each problem was magnified many times over.

Throughout the treatment, the therapist attempted to examine these difficulties from a variety of angles. For example, from an interpretive point of view, it became apparent that the patient's maddening habit of going into extreme detail stemmed from her childhood attempts to protect herself from being attacked by her mother for being stupid and wrong. She had felt compelled to summon massive evidence to buttress her position, even when on seemingly trivial matters. Although the patient could understand how this method of protecting herself tended to backfire and, in fact, elicit the very irritation she was hoping to avoid, the style nevertheless continued. The therapist also realized that the patient's need for detail was not unlike that of a young latency-age child who must give a parent every detail of something he or she is excited about. The patient herself realized that her speech difficulties, which had obvious sources in her own childhood, represented a severe and ongoing impediment to all interpersonal relationships. As she made progress in her treatment and contact with people became more important and less threatening to her, she independently sought out a speech therapist as well as classes in basic writing skills. Despite all of these efforts, from the therapist's perspective, very little headway was being made in correcting the speech difficulties within the therapy sessions.

Although there were islands of time within each session during which the therapist felt more involved and in contact with the patient, virtually every session contained long periods when the patient would burrow down into her nest of blankets and pillows, showing only her head, and then launch off on a lengthy soliloquy characterized by all of her speech and language problems. Despite the therapist's repeated attempts over the years to call attention to the interaction and to examine its possible precipitants and meanings, the soliloquies continued. Increasingly, the therapist found himself drifting away from the patient during these intervals and feeling less able to summon the enormous effort required to follow the patient's verbal reverie.

Eventually, it dawned on the therapist that his lifeless involvement with the patient at such times was suggestive of her propensity for stuffed animals, as though he himself had become their flesh-and-blood equivalent. Unlike those periods in every session when the therapist felt there was a genuine feeling of interaction with the patient, he gradually developed the clear impression that during her soliloquies the patient was oblivious to anything but his physical presence. She hardly seemed to notice, much less care, whether he was listening or not listening. Verbal interventions at such times seemed irrelevant or intrusive to her. The intervals of verbal reverie might last as long as 20 or 30 minutes at a stretch. The content invariably involved some event of the day, such as a business strategy, a phone conversation with her father, an interaction with a cab driver, or the like. Although the therapist would struggle valiantly to search for transference allusions and unconscious meanings to this material, interventions along these lines would result in the patient's politely listening but then gradually returning to what seemed to be something like a daily quota of verbal reverie.

The patient, however, never truly lost touch with reality during these intervals. She was always scrupulously aware of the time and would spontaneously begin to "pack up" near the end of each session. The point is that it just did not seem to matter one way or the other whether the therapist was animate or inanimate during such periods. And yet at other times during the same session, the patient might be receptive to interpretations, seek input, initiate or respond to humor, and generally seem more in contact with the therapist.

As the therapist found himself having to struggle more and more with feelings of intolerance, irritability, and even contempt for the patient, he also became progressively guilt-ridden for having this attitude. Informal consultation with colleagues was of little help. In attempting to understand the sources of his troubling countertransference attitude, he made great efforts over time to differentiate his own personal propensities from his responsiveness to the patient's power of inducing identifications. Although the therapist had not been aware of this attitude toward the patient in the first four or five years of treatment in other than an episodic way, his countertransference struggle was nevertheless something that gradually developed over an extended period of several years, making the current differentiation between his own contribution and the patient's that much more difficult.

THIS MATERIAL FORCEFULLY SUGGESTS THAT THE THERAPIST IS INDEED TRYING TO COPE WITH AN ENDURING COUNTERTRANSFERENCE ATTITUDE THAT HAS EVOLVED OVER SEVERAL YEARS. SUCH A COUNTERTRANSFERENCE EXPERIENCE IS TO BE DISTINGUISHED FROM THOSE REAC-

TIONS THAT ARE LESS FIXED AND MAY IN FACT BE RESPONSIVE TO A SINGLE, FLEETING INTERCHANGE. ALTHOUGH WE DISAGREE WITH THE TERMINOLOGY, THIS PHENOMENON HAS BEEN REFERRED TO AS A "COUNTERTRANSFERENCE NEUROSIS" AND IS SOMETIMES ASCRIBED SOLELY TO "THE THERAPIST'S PSYCHOPATHOLOGY." SCHEMATICALLY, THE THERAPIST APPEARS TO HAVE PROGRESSED THROUGH ALL PHASES AND SUBPHASES, YET CONTINUES TO STRUGGLE WITH POWERFUL SIGNAL AFFECTS OF INTOLERANCE, IRRITABILITY, AND CONTEMPT IN OPPOSITION TO STRONG GUILT FEELINGS. THE ABSENCE OF SPECIFICITY DOES NOT ALLOW FOR FURTHER SCHEMATIC COMMENT.

In one particular session, the difficulties that he and his patient were having with one another were very much in the forefront. The session occurred early on a Monday morning. The therapist was feeling tired and all too aware of the demands of a busy day and a busier week that lay ahead of him. Although he felt that his first two morning appointments had gone well and he was beginning to feel more "in the groove," the session with the patient in question no sooner had begun than the therapist found himself feeling stirred up. Even before the therapist had time to take his seat, the patient—grinning from ear to ear—proudly announced that she had received special recognition for performing best in her class on an assignment in a writing seminar for business professionals. The patient then paused, clearly looking to the therapist for some form of acknowledgment. The therapist was immediately aware of two opposing forces operating within himself. On one hand, he felt a pull to acknowledge her achievement and explore what it meant to her. Such an intervention would have been entirely consistent with the fabric of the treatment and commensurate with the patient's efforts to bridge the communicative gap between herself and other people. On the other hand, the therapist felt a flash of resentment, thinking, "Can't I even get in my chair before you start pulling on me for something?"

The therapist continued to be caught up in this inner conflict, when the critical moment for comment passed and the patient quickly moved on to other material. Although a quality of tension accompanied the remainder of the session, no further comment was made by the patient on the therapist's stony silence at a a time when some form of inquiry or acknowledgment was called for. He sensed that his unresponsiveness was clearly overdetermined and could not be dismissed on the grounds of "technical neutrality."

> THE FOREGOING MATERIAL STRONGLY SUGGESTS A DISRUPTION IN THE EMPATHIC PROCESS EVINCED BY THE THERAPIST'S FAILURE TO INTERVENE, EITHER IN AN EXPLORATORY OR SUPPORTIVE FASHION, AT A TIME WHEN AN INTERVENTION WAS CLEARLY CALLED FOR. IT APPEARS AT THE OUTSET OF THE SESSION THAT THE THERAPIST'S MENTAL SET WAS CLOUDED BY HIS FEELING TIRED AND OVERTAXED BY A BUSY SCHEDULE. THE PATIENT THEN EXERTED INTERACTIONAL PRESSURE BY HER NOT SO SUBTLE REQUEST FOR PRAISE, DELIVERED AT AN UNEXPECTED MOMENT, CATCHING THE THERAPIST BEFORE HE HAD GATHERED HIMSELF. THE SWIFTNESS OF THE THERAPIST'S INNER EMOTIONAL RESPONSIVENESS ATTESTS TO THE RELEVANCE OF THIS IMMEDIATE EPISODE FOR THE ONGOING COUNTERTRANSFERENCE PROBLEMS. THE POWERFUL SIGNAL AFFECT OF RESENTMENT INDICATES THE ACTIVATION OF AN IDENTIFICATION WITHIN THE THERAPIST THAT DOES NOT APPEAR TO HAVE BEEN WELL CONTAINED, GIVEN HIS WITHHOLDING OF AN INTERVENTION. WHETHER OR NOT PRAISE IS DELIVERED TO THE PATIENT, SOME EFFORT IS CALLED FOR HERE TO EXAMINE, AT THE VERY LEAST, THE PATIENT'S WISH FOR PRAISE.

In an effort to arrive at a better understanding of what he knew to be a reflection of his overall countertransference struggle with this patient, the therapist first tried to put himself in his patient's shoes. By actively imagining himself to be this patient at this particular time speaking to her therapist in this particular way, the "therapist-as-patient" was anxiously aware of a profound sense of dependency on the therapist, such that a stormy or disappointing session would unavoidably result in a very bad day. The sense of having no foundation with which to go out into life would continue until the damage with the therapist could be repaired. The therapist-as-patient was well aware that the reverse formula was also true, namely, that a feeling of being "well nourished" by the therapist would produce a sense of imperviousness to difficulties that might arise in life outside the therapy hour. At this very minute, the therapist-as-patient was aware that the session was not going well, that the therapist's failure to respond was accompanied by a deep sense of hurt and neglect, and that a feeling of panic was rising concerning the continuing negative momentum of the session. Furthermore, any effort seemed futile to try to ward off the feeling that the therapist, like her mother, really could not stand her and wished to sabotage her in every way possible.

The therapist then shifted his listening perspective in order to fathom his own reaction to the patient as fully as possible. In this particular set of circumstances, he realized that several factors must be contributing to his withholding stance with the patient. First, from long experience with the patient, he realized that his extreme annoyance was in fact very similar to what seemed to have been the patient's mother's subjective experience. He realized that gradually, over the years, the patient had in fact "gotten under his skin" and that, as her mother may have felt, he now felt extremely burdened by the symbiotic attachment that had been achieved in the therapeutic relationship. Though he recognized both the necessity of such an attachment and the benefit to the patient that had already accrued, her attachment nevertheless tended to feel more parasitic than symbiotic.

He realized that the patient's style of speech created a steady source of strain on his attentiveness. Despite her efforts to improve, he believed that her speech problems had in fact worsened as her therapeutic attachment had deepened. It was as though the patient, as if by magic, expected the therapist to understand her regardless of the lack of clarity in her speech. In its most extreme form, during her soliloquies, it did not even seem to matter if the therapist understood or not, just as long as he did not interfere with her imagining that he understood. Over time, this had come to grate on the therapist's nerves "like Chinese water torture," engendering feelings that echoed those of the patient's mother. Though the therapist never actually wished he could be rid of the patient once and for all, he recognized the features of this in his resentment of her for monopolizing certain session times that he wished he could offer to other patients who had busier schedules.

Following the session, the therapist continued to reflect on what had transpired. He realized that on this particular Monday morning his irritation and his withholding stance with the patient was partly a function of his feeling tired and generally burdened by the prospect of a long day and a longer week ahead. Although this temporary condition rendered him more reactive to his hostile impulses toward the patient, it did not explain the ongoing countertransference struggle. He became very aware of how hurt, angry, and afraid the patient felt because of his failure to respond to her wish for acknowledgment, and he found himself feeling a growing sense of guilt for having succumbed to his impatience by not responding affirmatively to the patient. This feeling of guilt had become very familiar to him in working with this patient over the years.

In considering how his own propensities entered into his countertransference problems with the patient, the therapist acknowledged a general personality trait characterized by a feeling of guilt that whatever he did was not quite good enough. Although he believed that in his own personal analysis he had succeeded in substantially reducing his tendency toward unwarranted guilt, he nevertheless saw evidence of this tendency surfacing in his work with certain patients. To see how his own guilt might be contributing to his response to this particular patient over an extended period, he asked himself what it was about his work with this particular patient that stimulated his own feelings of guilt. This morning's session provided a clear illustration—namely, momentary intolerance for the patient's childlike dependency.

But he also recognized a different element in the interaction that went beyond the issue of dependency. He had felt manipulated by the patient, which seemed to provide an important key to the way in which he often felt manipulated in more extreme forms by this patient. Suddenly it occurred to him that during the patient's periods of extended monologue, in which she seemed neither to care or notice whether he was listening or paying attention, he may well have felt manipulated into a state of lifelessness that did not seem to occur of his own volition. Efforts to explore the patient's need for the therapist to resemble a stuffed animal through transference interpretations had not altered the pattern in the slightest. The therapist now realized more clearly that, just as a teddy bear is manipulated by a child, he felt very much manipulated by this patient during her soliloquies and was deprived of any feeling of liveliness, initiative, or agency.

Although intellectually he recognized the necessity and usefulness of not interfering with the patient's need to "interact" with him in this manner on the way to developmentally more advanced object-relatedness, the *experience* of fulfilling this role for the patient over the years of the treatment had made the therapist very uncomfortable. With this discomfort came a twofold feeling of guilt. First, he felt guilty for resenting the patient for "killing me off like this" and for the resulting impulse to retaliate, for example, by withholding when she did "bring me back to life." Second, the therapist felt guilty for feeling that somehow he was not living up to his own internalized professional ideal; that is to say, he felt he should be actively listening, following, and interpreting, none of which seemed either possible or useful when his silent presence seemed to be all that mattered to the patient. He now saw much more clearly how his own guilt had inevitably contributed to his problems in tolerating the patient and maintaining an affirmative analytic attitude (Schafer, 1983) toward her.

THE THERAPIST HAS RESPONDED TO HIS REALIZATION OF AN EMPATHIC DISRUPTION WITH EXTENSIVE UTILIZATION OF THE PATIENT-INTERACTION AND THERAPIST-INTERACTION WORKING MODELS. IN SO DOING, HE SEEMS TO HAVE REGAINED GREATER TOLERANCE FOR THE PATIENT'S EXTREME DEPENDENCY AND TO HAVE UNDERSTOOD MORE EFFECTIVELY THE SOURCES AND MEANINGS OF HIS COUNTERTRANSFERENCE EXPERIENCE. THE IMMEDIATE INTERACTION WITH THE PATIENT HAS HELPED TO CLARIFY SOME OF THE UNDERLYING FACTORS IN THE ONGOING COUNTERTRANSFERENCE ATTITUDE THAT HAS EVOLVED OVER THE YEARS. ON ONE HAND, THE THERAPIST HAS COME TO UNDERSTAND THAT HIS ANNOYANCE AND INTOLERANCE FOR THE PATIENT AROSE IN PART FROM THE PATIENT'S PROJECTIVE IDENTIFICATION. THE PATIENT'S SPEECH DIFFICULTIES, ESPECIALLY HER BACKFIRING ATTEMPTS TO GO into extensive detail so as to avoid irritation from others, are experienced as "Chinese water torture," which slowly and insidiously induces an angry and withholding maternal identification. Similarly, the patient's apparent need for the therapist to become a silent teddy bear, who does not interfere by showing signs of life, represents a powerful and understandably stifling form of interactional pressure. On the other hand, the therapist has come to see more clearly the impact on his countertransference of his own propensity to feel guilty for drifting off, being unable to follow the patient's reverie, and being unable to tolerate the experience of what feels like manipulation. As Sandler (1976) has emphasized, the therapist's countertransference attitude appears to be a result of the therapist's propensities and the patient's unconscious re-creation of the past in the present, stirring up problematic feelings in the therapist. By silently formulating the manner in which his own experience and that of the patient form a complementarity, the therapist has progressed into the empathic connection subphase of internal processing.

Although the therapist had been unable to approach any of this material in the morning session, his hypothesis was confirmed that his failure to respond affirmatively to the patient's important achievement was upsetting and disorganizing for her. The confirmation came in the form of an extremely distressing phone message left on his answering machine shortly after the session. In the message, the patient sobbed hysterically and said that she could not understand why the therapist had not in some way acknowledged her writing award. She herself made the connection that she felt the therapist must hate her as she believed her mother had, since this was the only explanation that made any sense.

The therapist's formulation does indeed appear to be validated by the patient's overt display of distress and by the accompanying comparison of therapist to mother. This hypothesis as to the

BILATERAL SOURCES OF HIS COUNTERTRANSFERENCE EXPERIENCE RECEIVES VALIDATING SUPPORT FROM ALL FIVE LINES OF INFERENCE: OBSERVABLE FEATURES OF THE INTERACTION; THE COMPLEMENTARITY OF PATIENT-THERAPIST EXPERIENCE; THE PARADIGMATIC NATURE OF THE INTERACTION FOR THE PATIENT; THE PARADIGMATIC NATURE OF THE INTERACTION FOR THE THERAPIST; OTHER FACTORS (E.G., TIREDNESS) THAT COULD BE CONTRIBUTING. SIMILARLY, THE HYPOTHESIS THAT THE THERAPIST'S COUNTERTRANSFERENCE RESPONSE HAS UNCONSCIOUS MEANING FOR THE PATIENT DERIVES VALIDATING SUPPORT FROM THE SIMILARITY BETWEEN THE THERAPIST'S RESPONSE TO THE PATIENT AND THE REPORTED CONTEMPT OF THE PATIENT'S MOTHER FOR HER. THIS POWERFUL EVENT ALLOWS BOTH PATIENT AND THERAPIST TO EXPERIENCE FIRSTHAND THE TRAUMATIC PATTERN IN RELATIONSHIPS THAT IS MOST PROBLEMATIC FOR THE PATIENT. ACCESS TO THE PAST IS ACHIEVED BY ITS RE-CREATION IN THE PRESENT.

On the following day, the patient arrived for her session appearing both angry and afraid. The therapist then made the following interpretation:

T: I think I'm beginning to understand how upset you were yesterday that I did not seem pleased with you for your award. For whatever reasons, I agree with you that we were not really in synch when the session began. Because of that, I can see why you felt like I really let you down. I know that what goes on in here between you and me has a tremendous impact on you, literally from one session to the next. I fully understand how my behavior would have hit on some really sore spots for you.

After a brief silence during which the patient appeared to be absorbing the therapist's comment, she proceeded to expand upon the fact that the interaction during the previous session had indeed very much reminded her of her mother's hostile neglect. She went on to describe how she had either been too afraid to voice her disappointment directly to her mother, or, if she had spoken up, her mother would become furious. The patient then commented that she and her mother never had had the conciliatory contact that she and the therapist were now having.

THE THERAPIST HAS DELIVERED A TRANSFERENCE/COUNTERTRANSFERENCE-BASED COMMUNICATION TO THE PATIENT, EMPHASIZING THE COMPLEMENTARITY OF HIS OWN UNRESPONSIVENESS AND THE PATIENT'S CONSEQUENT DISTRESS. THE THERAPIST HAS CHOSEN, AT THIS PARTICULAR POINT IN TIME, NOT TO ENTER INTO THE VARIOUS FACTORS THAT APPEAR TO HAVE PRECIPITATED HIS UNRESPONSIVENESS. THE PATIENT HERSELF APPEARS TO CORROBORATE THE FORMULATION AND TO EXPAND ON THE GENETIC REVERBERATIONS. AS SHE POINTS OUT, THE EFFORTS AT REPAIRING THE EMPATHIC DISRUPTION CLEARLY SEEM TO DIFFERENTIATE THE PRESENT EXPERIENCE WITH THE THERAPIST FROM PAST EXPERIENCES WITH MOTHER.

After several minutes of exploring the similarities and differences between the current interaction with the therapist and the past relationship with mother, there was a lengthy silence. During the silence, the patient surrounded herself with her blankets and pillows. The silence was broken by an all too familiar monologue in which she described in extensive detail an interaction with a prospective client. The therapist immediately felt that his role in the interaction had been shifted by the patient. He was now the silent observer whose listening presence was all that was required. As the interaction continued, the therapist was aware of a renewed receptivity toward his assigned role and found listening to the content of the patient's monologue far more tolerable, at least for the time being.

THE CONCLUDING MATERIAL ILLUSTRATES THAT THE THERAPIST'S USEFUL EFFORTS IN EXAMINING HIS COUNTERTRANSFERENCE ATTITUDE DID NOT RESULT IN HIS BEING ABLE TO "ANALYZE AWAY" THE PATIENT'S PATTERN OF INTERACTING. IT IS AS THOUGH THE PATIENT IS SEEKING THE SOOTHING AND COMFORTING THAT SHE APPEARS TO DERIVE FROM HER SOLILOQUIES AS A FINAL STEP IN REPAIRING THE EMPATHIC DISRUPTION THAT HAS JUST TRANSPIRED. IT MIGHT HAVE BEEN INTERESTING TO SEE WHAT WOULD HAVE OCCURRED HAD THE THERAPIST ATTEMPTED TO INTERPRET THE PATIENT'S ENTERING INTO A MONOLOGUE AS A FINAL STEP IN RECOUPING FROM AN EMPATHIC DERAILMENT. WHETHER OR NOT SUCH AN INTERPRETATION WOULD HAVE BEEN USEFUL, IT IS CLEAR

THAT THE THERAPIST'S IMPROVED TOLERANCE AND HIS ENHANCED UNDERSTANDING OF THE INTERACTIONAL DYNAMICS ARE THE SALIENT BENEFITS OF ALL THAT HAS TRANSPIRED. IT MAY BE ANTICIPATED THAT SIMILAR COUNTERTRANSFERENCE FEELINGS WILL AGAIN ARISE, BUT THE THERAPIST MAY BE MORE EMPATHICALLY RESILIENT FOR HAVING BEEN THROUGH THIS WITH HIS PATIENT.

CASE 3. COUNTERTRANSFERENCE ALARM

The patient is a 43-year-old commercial artist in her fourth year of thrice weekly treatment. From the age of seven or eight until she left home for college, the patient, an only child, was a victim of ongoing sexual abuse by her father. Although the patient never entertained the notion that at some level her mother might actually have been aware of what was happening with father, mother was frequently present in the home during the episodes of abuse. The patient carried an unresolved burden of profound guilt and rage at her father into adulthood but could describe only a feeling of numbness toward her mother. At an early age, she married a distant, self-absorbed alcoholic who would become sexually abusive while intoxicated. The marriage produced two children, one now in college and the other working, both living out of state. When the patient was in her mid-30s, both parents committed suicide—father by hanging following a series of business failures, mother by overdose two weeks later. In response, the patient was aware only of feeling enormous guilt and a sense of somehow being responsible for their deaths.

Throughout the early years of the treatment, it became apparent to the therapist that the patient had an extremely difficult time with angry feelings, from which she consistently seemed to wall herself off. In addition, she characteristically turned anger toward herself in the form of intense self-depreciation. Rarely did she experience any respite from feelings of chronic depression and extreme guilt. She frequently worried that if she were to cross her husband in any way, he, too, would commit suicide. As a consequence, she never felt able to stand up to him for his cruel and demeaning treatment of both herself and their children. Described as an unhappy and unsuccessful accountant, he did indeed make periodic references to killing himself, thus intensifying the patient's trepidation and reinforcing the sadomasochistic paradigm.

Within the therapeutic interaction, the therapist believed that the patient had gained some insight into the connections between her relationship with her husband and her relationship with her father. These insights seemed genuine and hard won, and the patient gradually became more assertive with her husband and less self-depreciative. Nevertheless, the therapist felt consistently foiled in his attempts to interpret negative feelings on the patient's part toward himself. Even when there appeared to be clearcut evidence that feelings of anger and disappointment were present, interpretations to that effect (e.g., "I think you are disappointed in me right now") were vigorously denied. A similar fate was suffered by interpretations of the patient's self-protective resistance even to the awareness of negative feelings directed at the therapist (e.g., "I think it frightens you even to think that you might be disappointed with me"). Typically, the patient would respond with comments like, "Now don't take this personally, but I just don't think you have that much impact on me that I could ever really feel angry with you. You're just trying to do your job."

With a rapidity and abruptness that surprised the therapist, the apparent pattern of massive denial of negative transference seemed to shift virtually overnight. Previously the patient had expressed some frustration with what she experienced as the slow progress of the treatment. But despite the therapist's attempts to illuminate negative transference, the patient had insisted that only she herself was to blame. Then, without warning, she arrived for a session and immediately erupted with anger toward the therapist. With references to her husband's drunken abusiveness and to feelings of exploitation at the hands of her employer and co-workers, she spoke more loudly and angrily than ever before:

P: I have no idea what I'm supposed to be doing here. All I know is that I am sick and tired of everyone fucking with me. I come in here and I'm forced to humiliate myself in front of you, telling you about all the ugly, disgusting things happening in my life and what a miserable failure I am at doing anything about it. And you just sit there!

T: (attempting to recover from his surprise at the suddenness and intensity of the patient's fury and distress, responding in a very controlled tone) You seem pretty angry with me.

P: (harshly and loudly) Now you're getting the idea! I come in here week after week begging for help with my wretched little life and I'm about at the end of my rope. I don't think you have any idea at all of just how hard it is for me. Everywhere I turn, people are fucking me over—my husband, my boss, the other people in the office. You never say anything to guide me. All you do is sit there—cool, calm, and collected. Every now and then, you try to poke around in what you say is my unconscious, and I don't even know if such a thing really exists. But I know that whatever you're doing, it's not working for me. You have to *do* something!

THE PATIENT'S SUDDEN VERBAL ATTACK REPRESENTS HEAVY INTERACTIONAL PRESSURE, WHICH IS INTENSIFIED BY THE FACT THAT IT COMES AS A COMPLETE SURPRISE TO THE THERAPIST.

The patient continued in this vein for several minutes. The therapist noted in himself a mounting sense of alarm, both because of the suddenness of the patient's wrath and because of the potential allusion to suicide, given her father's death by hanging ("I'm about at the end of my rope"). Listening to his own voice as he interacted with the patient, the therapist became aware of increasing control in his tone. His words were so carefully selected and his delivery so polished that he observed himself beginning to sound as though he were reading from a script. As the session progressed, the therapist became more aware of his highly controlled manner with the patient—never fumbling for a word, never deviating from an almost pleasant tone of voice. At the same time, the patient's fury with the therapist escalated to the point that he felt genuinely alarmed about her suicidal potential as she left the office in view of her obvious level of disorganization and distress.

THE SIGNAL AFFECT OF ALARM SUGGESTS THAT THE THERAPIST HAS INDEED RESPONDED TO THE PATIENT'S PROJECTIVE IDENTIFICATION. IN ATTEMPTING TO CONTAIN AND SEPARATE FROM THE IDENTIFICATION THAT HAS BEEN INTROJECTED, HE IS AWARE OF HAVING TO COMPENSATE FOR AN INNER SENSE OF FEELING OUT OF CONTROL BY AN

> OUTWARD PRESENTATION THAT IS EXCESSIVELY CONTROLLED. THE PRESENTATION OF EXTREME SELF-CONTROL ON THE THERAPIST'S PART IN TURN APPEARS TO INFLAME THE PATIENT'S WRATH, SUCH THAT A WIDENING POLARIZATION APPEARS TO BE DEVELOPING. THUS, IT APPEARS THAT THE THERAPIST IS STRUGGLING WITH THE TASKS OF THE SEPARATION-CONTAINMENT SUBPHASE AND THAT HIS CONTROLLED DEMEANOR REPRESENTS A DEFENSIVE ACTING OUT OF HIS SENSE OF ALARM.

Following the session, the therapist felt so unglued that he sought immediate consultation. In reviewing the case and especially the events of the most recent session, the therapist attempted to make sense of his own countertransference experience in relation to what the patient seemed to be experiencing. Several hypotheses emerged from the consultative process.

First, the therapist's experience of the patient's tirade as being sudden, abrupt, uncontrollable, and totally unanticipated seemed reminiscent of what the patient had recounted as her own childhood experience of her father's sexual assault. Just as the patient remembered having become dissociatively stiff, rigid, and unfeeling in her terror and confusion at father's shocking behavior, similarly the therapist had "frozen up" in response to the patient's alarming and confusing attack. Thus, the therapist entertained the possibility that, with role reversal, the patient had induced in him an experience similar to her own experience of childhood sexual abuse. At the same time, the patient was transiently identifying with aspects of the abusive paternal introject, a formulation that was further supported by the comment, "I feel as though I am at the end of my rope."

In trying to understand how his own tendencies had come into play in the interaction, the therapist was aware of his inclination to become highly controlled under circumstances of stress, especially in response to aggressive or threatening behavior by others. He realized that his own response to the patient's aggressiveness could have perpetuated a further polarization, infuriating the patient, in her embarrassment and exasperation, even more.

Second, the therapist entertained the possibility that the patient was experiencing the overall treatment itself as a recapitulation of father's sexual abuse. Clearly, the patient felt exposed, humiliated, and forced to display "ugly, disgusting" aspects of herself, while the therapist episodically "poked around" in her unconscious, leaving the patient feeling confused and awful about herself.

The third formulation, however, seemed most immediate and persuasive to the therapist. There was considerable evidence to suggest that the patient's fury with the therapist regarding his "just sitting there" and not helping, while the patient bitterly complained that "everyone is fucking with me," represented a reenactment of the patient's repressed fury with mother for not protecting her from father's sexual exploitation. Unlike in the experience with mother, however, in the current scenario the patient was fully conscious of her rage with the therapist for his perceived passivity. The therapist realized that his own tendency to become tightly controlled was central to the patient's perception of him as passive, detached, and ineffectual.

THE REVIEW OF THE INTERACTION THROUGH THE PATIENT-INTERACTION AND THERAPIST-INTERACTION WORKING MODELS ALLOWED THE THERAPIST TO ESTABLISH SEVERAL HYPOTHESES ABOUT THE POTENTIAL CONNECTION BETWEEN HIS OWN AND THE PATIENT'S EXPERIENCE. ALL THREE OF THE THERAPIST'S HYPOTHESES SUGGEST A COMPLEMENTARY RELATIONSHIP BETWEEN THE PATIENT AND THERAPIST, AND OFFER A DYNAMIC MEANING EMBEDDED IN THE REENACTMENT OF TRAUMATIC PATTERNS OF RELATING TO PARENTAL FIGURES. THE THERAPIST'S EFFORTS ARE SLIDING BACK AND FORTH BETWEEN THE WORKING MODEL AND EMPATHIC CONNECTION SUBPHASE. THE "TIME OUT" FROM THE HEAT OF THE THERAPEUTIC INTERACTION PROVIDED BY THE CONSULTATIVE PROCESS ALLOWED THE THERAPIST THE OPPORTUNITY TO EXAMINE THE VALIDATION CRITERIA SUPPORTING EACH OF HIS FORMULATIONS. EACH OF THE THERAPIST'S SOURCE HYPOTHESES RECEIVED VALIDATING SUPPORT FROM ALL FIVE LINES OF INFERENCE: EVIDENCE FROM THE IMMEDIATE INTERACTION; A CLEAR COMPLEMENTARY CORRESPONDENCE

BETWEEN PATIENT AND THERAPIST EXPERIENCE; HISTORICAL PARALLELS FOR THE PATIENT; AND SITUATIONAL AS WELL AS CHARACTEROLOGICAL ACKNOWLEDGMENT OF THE CONTRIBUTION OF THE THERAPIST'S OWN "PERSONAL EQUATION." VALIDATION FOR THE THERAPIST'S THREE FORMULATIONS WAS ALSO SUPPLIED BY THE CONVERGENCE OF SEVERAL LINES OF INFERENCE UNDER THE CATEGORY OF MEANING HYPOTHESES: IN THE REPETITION OF PAST RELATIONSHIP PATTERNS FOR THE PATIENT, UNCONSCIOUS COMMUNICATION TO THE THERAPIST, AND THE RESPONSE TO AN IMMEDIATE ADAPTIVE CONTEXT (THERAPIST'S EXTREME SELF-CONTROL).

With these formulations in mind, the therapist found himself feeling much less confused and alarmed. By feeling that he had a clearer understanding of what both he and the patient might be experiencing, he found himself actually looking forward to the next session. Though he was still somewhat apprehensive about the patient's safety from self-destructive urges, the consultation served the very important function of helping him to regain a sense of perspective. Once again, he felt he had the tools to help the patient sort through what was unfolding in the interaction.

ADDITIONAL VALIDATION FOR THE THERAPIST'S FORMULATION IS PROVIDED BY THE THERAPIST'S INCREASED UNDERSTANDING AND APPRECIATION OF THE PATIENT'S MOTIVATION, RENEWING HIS OBSERVATIONAL PERSPECTIVE, AND BROADENING HIS OWN SELF-KNOWLEDGE.

To the extent that the third formulation was valid, the therapist realized that the current phase of treatment offered an opportunity to bring to light the patient's long-buried rage with mother, targeted at the therapist because of the features of the current therapeutic interaction, which closely resembled the childhood scenario. Furthermore, there existed the potential to work toward a more effective integration of aggressive feelings without becoming overwhelmed. The therapist also recognized the danger that the current therapeutic interaction, poorly handled, could sadly reaffirm for the patient her conviction that people are not to be relied upon and that one must choose between total disavowal of angry, aggressive, self-assertive feelings on one hand and becoming destructively overwhelmed by them on the other.

Equipped with a renewed sense of perspective, the therapist found the patient arriving for the next session appearing decidedly depressed and reticent and speaking in a flat, subdued tone of voice. In content, she focused on how awful she felt about herself, saying that she could do nothing right. No mention whatsoever was made of her animosity toward the therapist for what she perceived as his failure to help her in an active and effective way. Placing himself in the patient's shoes, the therapist recognized not only her sense of guilt, but, more important, her sense of danger that, by attacking the therapist, she would in some way either psychologically kill him off or provoke an enraged retaliation.

THE THERAPIST'S REEMPLOYMENT OF THE PATIENT-INTERACTION WORKING MODEL SEEMS TO PROVIDE ADDITIONAL EMOTIONAL KNOWLEDGE AND VALIDATION FOR THE PRIOR FORMULATIONS.

Just as she had felt responsible for the suicides of her parents, perhaps now she was fearful that the therapist—even though physically present—would similarly be destroyed and would no longer be available emotionally to her. After a few minutes, the therapist felt increasingly convinced of the merit of this formulation. Prompted by what seemed to be the patient's deepening depression, he made the following interventions.

T: If I'm not mistaken, I think the way you seem to be feeling today is in response to how angry you were with me last time. I think you are worried about the effect all of that has had on me—whether I'm going to want to strike back, whether I will withdraw from you, or whether your anger with me has made me hate myself. I think that today, you've gone back to blaming yourself for everything. As unhappy as that makes you, I think that at least it feels safer to you than blaming me.

THE THERAPIST'S INTERVENTION, IN WHICH HE BEGINS TO LAY OUT A VARIETY OF POTENTIAL MEANINGS TO THE PATIENT OF HER ACTIONS, FALLS UNDER THE HEADING OF TRANSFERENCE-BASED COMMUNICATION, THE SECOND

SUBPHASE WITHIN THE COMMUNICATION PHASE. ALTHOUGH THE THERAPIST'S INTERNAL PROCESSING OF THE INTERACTION INCLUDES COUNTERTRANSFERENCE MATERIAL, HE HAS NOT YET ELECTED TO MAKE THAT EXPLICIT FOR OBVIOUS REASONS OF TIMING.

Following a long pause, the patient briefly made eye contact for the first time in the session, before again averting her glance. Very quietly, the patient replied, "Could be. I don't see what's to be gained by blaming you for my problems. How can that help?"

Feeling encouraged by the patient's response and the accompanying sense of enhanced contact, the therapist decided that the time might be ripe for the following:

T: Given how unhappy you are with the way your life is going, it's understandable to me that you would be pretty upset with me, since I'm the one that you're coming to for help. I think it is especially tough for you when you come in here and spill your guts and I then come across like "Mr. Cool, Calm, and Collected." I think that makes you feel like I'm not really involved with you, that I'm not really paying attention to how badly things are going, because if I were, I wouldn't seem so calm and it would feel more like I was coming down off my high horse and really trying to *do* something concrete and useful.

P: (after a pause, quietly) I guess I know you don't mean it to be that way, but that is how I feel.

T: Last time, you said that the thing about me that really infuriated you was that I was just sitting back while everyone was "fucking" with you. I believe those were your words. I've been thinking that your choice of words there may help us to understand better why you are so upset by what you experience as my passivity.

P: (brief pause) You mean the stuff with my father? I don't see your point.

T: (gently) Not just the stuff with your father. I'm referring to the stuff with your father *while* your mother sat back and did nothing.

P: (long pause, quietly) But she didn't know.

T: Even if we assume for the moment that she did not, on any level, know what was going on, would that not imply that she really wasn't paying attention? We're not talking about a single instance.

P: (angrily) So what are you saying, that my problem with you is all in my head, that it's really just my mother that I'm mad at?

T: It is definitely not my intention to say that your anger with me is some figment of your imagination. I agree that my style can be pretty controlled and unemotional at times. In addition, many of the problems for which you came to me to get help continue to be painful for you. Given those two points, I think my failure to seem more active and effective with you opens up a very old and very aching wound for you that makes your disappointments with me that much more difficult to bear.

THE PATIENT'S RECEPTIVITY TO THE EARLIER INTERVENTION IN CONJUNCTION WITH THE THERAPIST'S SENSE OF ENHANCED CONTACT PROVIDES ADDITIONAL POSTINTERPRETIVE VALIDATION. THIS HAS LAID THE GROUNDWORK FOR THE MORE AMBITIOUS TRANSFERENCE/COUNTERTRANSFERENCE-BASED COMMUNICATION. THE THERAPIST IS FACING THE CHALLENGING TASK OF EXAMINING THE PATIENT'S EXPERIENCE NEITHER AS A "DISTORTION" NOR AS UNINFLUENCED BY THE PAST, BUT RATHER AS A PLAUSIBLE CONSTRUAL BASED UPON BOTH PAST AND PRESENT.

P: I don't know. I just don't know what to think. My father had such a horrible temper. What could my mother have done anyway? (long pause) I know that when my husband treats the kids like shit, I hate myself for not being able to stand up for them. It just feels like it's bad enough they're not getting a fair shake from him without making it worse by having a mouse for a mother. So if I'm upset with myself now because of the kids, maybe I've been more angry with my mother than I've let myself know. I don't know. It's all just so confusing.

At this juncture, the therapist felt that he and the patient were no longer at odds. Though the underlying issues were in no way resolved, the therapist felt he genuinely understood his patient much better than he had previously. The patient now had had the experience of becoming intensely angry with her therapist without disastrous consequences. For this reason, the therapist believed that the alliance had been strengthened. Regarding the patient's repressed feelings toward her own mother, some work had been done toward bringing those feelings closer to consciousness and making them more accessible to therapeutic influence.

11 *Closing Comments*

IN THIS FINAL CHAPTER, we would like to look back over the territory we have covered and emphasize the salient points that have been made.

Our examination of the unitary sequence for the therapist's processing of interactional communications from the patient has served to elaborate our view that when empathy occurs, projective identification is always involved. The experience of empathy on the therapist's part always involves the reception and processing of a projective identification transmitted by the patient. Previous examinations of empathy have not sufficiently recognized that the empathic trial identification, whether concordant or complementary, that takes place within the therapist during the empathic process is an experiential state induced through the interaction with the patient. Empathy in the therapist does not take place in isolation, nor is it primarily an intrapsychic phenomenon. Empathy is the *outcome* of a radically mutual interactive process between patient and therapist in which the therapist receives and processes projective identifications from the patient. This formulation is applicable to projective identifications from the patient that are difficult to contain and that involve considerable introspective work on the therapist's part as well as substantial pressure from the patient, as in the vignettes detailed in chapter 10. This formulation also applies to easily and smoothly processed projective identifications involving minimal work by the therapist and little or no pressure from the patient.

Similarly, concordant and complementary are terms describing the structural arrangement of the identification within the therapist as it bears a relationship to the patient's immediately experienced self- and object representation. These terms are independent of any assessment of the ease or difficulty in the therapist's experience of the identification. If one recognizes that the type of identification (concordant or complementary) and the experience of processing that identification are two independent dimensions, then one will not draw the erroneous conclusions that the therapist's reception of a projective identification always involves a complementary identification that is difficult to experience and, conversely, that empathy always involves a concordant identification that is comfortably experienced by the therapist. Central to our thesis is the view that the reception of a projective identification may involve either concordant *or* complementary trial identifications in the therapist, and the experience of either type of identification may be difficult or comfortable.

In projective identification, then, there is always the potential for empathy, whether or not this potential is actualized. In the reception and processing of a projective identification from the patient, there is always the potential for the therapist to process the projective identification successfully to the point where an empathic understanding of the patient is attained. All successful processing of projective identifications will ultimately result in concordant empathic knowledge of the patient. An initial complementary identification experienced by the therapist, if managed properly, will lead to an understanding that is concordant with the patient's experience. In this manner, all empathic knowledge in its final form may be considered concordant. The path toward this final empathic outcome may begin for the therapist with either a complementary or concordant introjective identification.

We are in essential agreement with those who view projective identification as an unconscious attempt to communicate with the therapist in a manner potentially much more powerful than words alone. Yet, as our examination of the three phases of processing interactional communications has demonstrated, there is the serious possibility for breakdown at any point along the line, resulting in a failure to actualize the communicative potential of the projective identification. For example, the therapist's trial identification with either a concordant or complementary aspect of the patient's internal world may strike too close to home for the therapist or, conversely, may be too remote from the therapist's repertoire of experiences of self. The therapist in these instances may impulsively react to the feeling of interactional pressure from the patient during the Reception phase by attempting to "fight fire with fire." Similarly, the therapist may not be able to tolerate a temporary sense of himself as hopeless, incompetent, furious, hateful, terrified, and the like. On the other hand, a therapist may overidentify with a patient's need to see him as extraordinarily powerful, wise, or gifted. Throughout our presentation of the schema, we have provided guidelines to the potential disruptions that can occur as the empathic process unfolds.

Our understanding of projective identification and empathy contradicts the notion that they are congruent and individually based operations, with the therapist engaging in empathy and the patient engaging in projective identification. We understand both patient and therapist to be mutually involved in the operation of projective identification—the former as the initiator and the latter as the recipient of the identification. Klein's (1946) original use of the term referred only to an intrapsychic mechanism with no impact on the interpersonal world of real external objects. But like many others who have extended the term projective identification as a bridging concept between the intrapsychic and interpersonal spheres, we take the position that one cannot speak of projective identification from the patient without addressing introjective identification within the therapist. Along the same lines, empathy is the outcome in the therapist of a radically mutual and interactive experience between patient and therapist. Two conclusions should be evident from this view: first, both participants are always *mutually* engaged when the operations of projective identification and empathy occur; and, second, these two operations are not congruent, but rather consecutive, in their occurrence.

Several authors have addressed the clinical significance of the operations of empathy and projective identification for the patient's intrapsychic functioning, the stability of the therapeutic relationship, and the therapist's own personal growth. The therapist's continuous working through of projective identifications from the patient toward an empathic outcome offers the patient the opportunity, through the corrective object relationship, to strengthen ego integration by the introjection of a more tolerant view of negative self-representations (Jaffee, 1968; Beres and Arlow, 1974; Meissner, 1980). This capacity on the therapist's part also strengthens the therapeutic relationship as it is experienced by both patient and therapist (Racker, 1957; Schafer, 1959; Beres and Arlow, 1974; Meissner, 1980). And it further affords the *therapist* the opportunity for potential growth within his own personality structure as a result of the consistent working and reworking of the projective identifications he receives from the patient (Schafer, 1959; Winnicott, 1965; Searles, 1975; Langs, 1978). The sequence of phases outlined examines this process under optimal and disrupted conditions.

We disagree with those authors (Langs, 1976; Ogden, 1979, 1982) who view success or failure in the processing of projective identifications in what appear to be very black and white terms. In contrast to their oversimplified view of *either* success *or* failure in a therapist's handling of a patient's projective identifications, we suggest that this is a complicated process characterized by relative degrees of success and failure. It follows that a theoretical and clinical model based on a continuum of relative degrees of success and failure is both more accurate and more clinically useful than a black-or-white, "yes-no" perspective. Our schema provides just such a framework for pinpointing the varieties of empathic arrests and regressions that can arise in the development of a therapist's empathic understanding.

Throughout this volume, we have attempted to extend the totalist tradition within countertransference theory, which states that Freud's characterization of transference as both "the greatest danger and the best tool for analytic work" (Racker, 1957) applies equally well to countertransference. In so doing, we have also striven to heed the caveat of the classical view of countertransference (Reich, 1951), which warns against the reflexive conclusion that a given countertransference response necessarily helps us to understand the patient. We have addressed the obvious need for a validating methodology by proposing five lines of inference for attempting to establish the source and the meanings of a given countertransference response. Although the interpretation of clinical material—countertransference-based or otherwise—does not lend itself to irrefutable proof, it is nevertheless both possible and necessary to examine emerging hypotheses in an organized and systematic fashion. By seeking convergence among the discrete lines of inference, the therapist is able to accomplish this task.

Similarly, there are no clearcut guidelines to the advisability and timing of countertransference disclosure, unless one takes the position at either extreme—that is, "never" versus "whenever the spirit moves you." Having found neither extreme to be satisfactory, we have delineated criteria by which interventions involving countertransference disclosure can be evaluated with respect to their preparation, implementation, and ultimate impact. These provide a framework from which to assess the usefulness or the disruptiveness of a countertransference disclosure before, during, and after its delivery.

With regard to the critical question of the teachability of empathy, our position is strongly affirmative. Greenson (1960) took up this question and concluded that although the "capacity for empathy" could not be taught, it was possible to remove or "cure" a disorder or "misuse" of empathy. As previously mentioned, he outlined two categories of disturbances of empathy in the therapist: inhibition and loss of control. He went no further in specifying what he meant by the "capacity for empathy," but it seems evident that he was referring to the variety of personality characteristics in the potential therapist that enhance the ability to entertain and observe trial identifications with the patient. For personality characteristics causing a restriction in the empathic capacity, a personal analysis or insight-oriented psychotherapy is commonly recommended.

Although we concur in the strongest possible terms with the need for personal psychotherapy or analysis in the preparation and training of therapists, we are aware of an all too common practice in clinical circles of attributing therapeutic "failures" to the therapist's need for more or better treatment in order to handle countertransference more effectively. The assumptions underlying this practice are twofold: that there is one primary cause for empathic disturbances (personality characteristics of the therapist), and that there is only one prescriptive method (treatment) applicable to the resolution of this problem.

The strongest adherent to this position is Robert Langs, whose voluminous writings are grounded in an examination of the uncontrolled "madness" of psychotherapists, which becomes manifest in the therapeutic interaction. At the other extreme are those who place the onus for difficult countertransference reactions exclusively on the sickness of the patient, who is often viewed as "untreatable," "acting out," or "resistant." Indeed, Langs's position may be interpreted as an extreme reaction to those who "blame" the patient. Although his approach is ostensibly set in a mutually interactive bipersonal field, Langs adheres to an essentially unidimensional perspective on countertransference difficulties by limiting his understanding of these reactions to an emphasis on the emotional deficits of the psychotherapist.

Returning to the question of the teachability of empathy, we believe that some treatments founder not because of the "madness" of the therapist or the untreatability of the patient, but rather as a consequence of empathic disruption in which the therapist fails in some critical way to understand the communicative meaning of the patient's words and actions. Therapeutic insight and understanding in such cases is usually replaced by the therapist's destructive reaction. Typically, the problems within the therapy represent an unfortunate recapitulation for the patient of some variant of the vicious circle in human relationships that brought him to treatment in the first place. We propose that our schema for the processing of interactional communications for an empathic outcome represents an effort to map out, in clear and specific terms, where the critical pitfalls lie. It represents movement forward from the global critique often heard in such cases of countertransference difficulty that the therapist needs more therapy. Although we agree that there are many cases in which a therapist *does indeed* need to seek personal treatment, there are also many cases in which the issue is didactic, conceptual, and cognitive and has much less to do with the therapist's personality structure than with his inadequate knowledge of how to process interactional communications.

There is a good deal about empathy that is indeed teachable. Our clinical and supervisory experience strongly indicates that if a therapist understands more effectively *why* he might be thinking and feeling as he is thinking and feeling with a particular patient, this can be put to very good use in furthering treatment. Such empathic understanding can then lay the groundwork for interpretations that, in turn, pave the way for vicious circles in the therapeutic interaction to be understood and worked through rather than merely repeated. Our schema establishes a framework for understanding more clearly the interactional meanings both of powerful countertransference experiences and of the more ordinary, moment-to-moment responsive flow of thoughts, feelings, associations, and impulses within the therapist in his day-to-day functioning. With regard to the widely accepted view that empathy consists of two component processes, our schema not only facilitates the second component, objective scrutiny of what one is experiencing, but in so doing, also broadens the therapist's receptivity to trial identifications, the initial component of empathy. Receptivity is increased because firmer understanding enhances therapeutic confidence, diminishes defensive activity on the therapist's part to otherwise objectionable self-experiences, and improves openness to the patient's influence.

A similar line of reasoning holds with respect to a second important question; namely, what are the implications of this schema for technique? Once again, irrespective of the extent to which one emphasizes interpretations dealing primarily with immediate transference material as opposed to genetic or current extratransference material, if a therapist has a clearer understanding of what he is experiencing and how that might be useful, he is in a much better position to implement whatever technique he happens to favor.

We wish to emphasize again that empathy, projective identification, and countertransference are concepts that bridge the intrapsychic and interpersonal realms of experience. We concur with Gill (1984) and Ogden (1979) that, because of the critical implications such concepts hold for the practice of psychoanalytic therapy, psychoanalytic theory and practice need to devote greater attention to the investigation and development of concepts that serve this bridging function. Three new concepts have been introduced: the therapist-interaction working model, the patient-interaction working model, and the interactional introject. The first two represent an expansion of Greenson's (1960) term, working model; the third refers to the internalized structure within the therapist formed by the conjunction of both working models. It is our position that these concepts clarify not only what occurs *within* the therapist, but also what unfolds *between* therapist and patient.

Bollas (1987) has proposed the term "extractive introjection," referring to an intersubjective procedure whereby one individual essentially "steals for a certain period of time (from a few seconds or minutes to a lifetime) an element of another individual's psychic life" (p. 158). An example might be a person who takes over responsibility for the decision that another has to make, such that the second person experiences himself as having no decision-making capabilities whatsoever. Bollas points out that extractive introjection both overlaps with what has been termed projective identification and at times represents its complement. The introduction of this term stands as an important attempt to develop a lexicon for those processes which bridge the intrapsychic and interpersonal realms.

Looking back, we recognize that by design we have focused virtually all of our attention on the experience of the therapist-in-interaction. We feel strongly that much could be gained by shifting the spotlight to the experience of the patient-in-interaction. Within the processing and validating frameworks we have delineated, it might be possible to examine the patient's experience from a fresh, new perspective. To what extent may it be said that the patient is a recipient of the therapist's projective identification? What can be said about how a patient processes the therapist's influence? How does this compare to the therapist's processing of the patient's influence? How does the patient seek to validate his perceptions of the therapist? In clinical consultation and supervision, to what extent do the processes we have outlined pertain to the supervisor-in-interaction with the supervisee. How might this perspective lead to more effective supervision?

Within our general focus on the therapist's experience, several lines of further inquiry suggest themselves. Can more be said about the factors that help the therapist establish the "psychological distance" necessary for the successful processing of an induced identification? How does the therapist decide whether to utilize direct versus indirect countertransference disclosure? Finally, the patient-interaction working model implies that the therapist listens to the patient's material as if the therapist were the patient. What are the qualitative differences in the associations produced by this listening model and the model often cited as "empathic," in which the therapist listens as if he were himself in the patient's "shoes"?

In closing, we return to the fundamental proposition that psychoanalytic psychotherapy is a process in which the therapist is susceptible to the full range of human emotions. We hope to have clarified the pathways and pitfalls for the therapist who seeks to draw upon his emotional responsiveness to the patient as a vivid source of understanding rather than as a destructive black mark on his objectivity.

References

Alexander, F. (1935) The problem of psychoanalytic technique. *Psychoanalytic Quarterly*, 4:588–611.

Balint, M. (1937) Early developmental states of the ego. In: *Primary Love and Psychoanalytic Technique*. New York: Liveright, 1965.

Balint, M. (1968) *The Basic Fault*. London: Tavistock.

Basch, M. F. (1983) Empathic understanding: A review of the concept and some theoretical considerations. *Journal of the American Psychoanalytic Association*, 34:101–126.

Benedek, T. (1953) Dynamics of the countertransference. *Bulletin of the Menninger Clinic*, 17:201–265.

Beres, D. & Arlow, J. A. (1974) Fantasy and identification in empathy. *Psychoanalytic Quarterly*, 43:26–50.

Berman, L. (1949) Countertransferences and attitudes of the analyst in the therapeutic process. *Psychiatry*, 12:159–166.

Bion, W. R. (1955) Language and the schizophrenic. In: *New Directions in Psychoanalysis*, ed. M. Klein, P. Heiman, & R. E. Money-Kyrle. London: Tavistock, pp. 220–239.

——— (1959) Attacks on linking. *International Journal of Psycho-Analysis*, 40:308–315.

Bollas, C. (1983) Expressive uses of the countertransference. *Contemporary Psychoanalysis*, 19:1–34.

——— (1987) *The Shadow of the Object*. New York: Columbia University Press.

Buie, D. H. (1981) Empathy: Its nature and limitations. *Journal of the American Psychoanalytic Association*, 29:281–307.

Burke, W. F. & Tansey, M. J. (1985) Projective identification and countertransference turmoil: Disruptions in the empathic process. *Contemporary Psychoanalysis*, 21:372–402.

Chediak, C. (1979) Counter-reactions and countertransference. *International Journal of Psycho-Analysis*, 60:117–129.

Cohen, M. B. (1952) Countertransference and anxiety. *Psychiatry*, 15:231–243.

Cutler, R. L. (1958) Countertransference effects in psychotherapy. *Journal of Consulting Psychology*, 22:349–356.

Deutsch, J. (1926) Occult processes occurring during psychoanalysis. In: *Psychoanalysis and the Occult*, ed. G. Devereux. New York: International Universities Press, 1953, pp. 133–146.

Edelson, M. (1984) *Hypothesis and Evidence in Psychoanalysis*. Chicago: University of Chicago Press.

Eissler, K. R. (1953) The effect of the structure of the ego on psychoanalytic technique. *Journal of the American Psychoanalytic Association*, 1:104–143.

Epstein, L. & Feiner, A. (1979) *Countertransference*. New York: Aronson.

Erikson, E. (1958) The nature of clinical evidence. *Deadalus*, 87:65–87.

Fairbairn, W. R. D. (1946) Object-relationships and dynamic structures. In: *An Object-Relations Theory of Personality*. New York: Basic Books, 1952.

Ferenczi, S. (1919) On the technique of psychoanalysis In: *Further Contributions to the Technique of Psychoanalysis*. London: Hogarth Press, 1950, pp. 177–188.

Finnell, J. S. (1986) The merits and problems with the concept of projective identification. *Psychoanalytic Review*, 73: 103–128.

Flarsheim, A. (1972) Treatability. In: *Tactics and Technique in Psychoanalytic Psychotherapy*, ed. P. L. Giovacchini. New York: Science House, pp. 113–134.

Fliess, R. (1942) The metapsychology of the analyst. *Psychoanalytic Quarterly*, 11:211–227.

——— (1953) Countertransference and counteridentification. *Journal of the American Psychoanalytic Association*, 1:268–284.

French, T. (1958) The art and science of psychoanalysis. *Journal of the American Psychoanalytic Association*, 6:197–214.

Freud, S. (1910) The future prospects of psychoanalytic therapy. *Standard Edition*, 11:141–151. London: Hogarth Press, 1953.

——— (1912) Recommendations to physicians practicing psycho-analysis. *Standard Edition*, 12:111–120. London: Hogarth Press, 1953.

——— (1913) The claims of psycho-analysis to the interest of the nonpsychological sciences. *Standard Edition*, 13:165–190. London: Hogarth Press, 1959.

——— (1914) Remembering, repeating, and working through. *Standard Edition*, 12:146–156. London: Hogarth Press, 1953.

——— (1937) Analysis terminable and interminable. *Standard Edition*, 23:209–253. London: Hogarth Press, 1953.

Fromm, E. (1941) *Escape from Freedom*. New York: Avon.

——— (1947) *Man for Himself*. Greenwich, CT: Fawcett.

——— (1955) *The Sane Society*. Greenwich, CT: Fawcett.

Gill, M. M. (1983) The interpersonal paradigm and the degree of the therapist's involvement. *Contemporary Psychoanalysis*, 19:200–237.

——— (1984) Discussion of "Projection and projective identification: Developmental and clinical aspects," by O. Kernberg. Presented at annual meeting of the American Psychoanalytic Association, December 21.

Giovacchini, P. L. (1972a) The analytic setting and the treatment of psychosis. In: *Tactics and Techniques in Psychoanalytic Psychotherapy*, ed. P. L. Giovachinni. New York: Science House, pp. 222–235.

——— (1972b) Technical difficulties in treating some characterological disorders: countertransference problems. *International Journal of Psychoanalytic Psychotherapy*, 1:112–128.

Goldberg, A. (1988) *A Fresh Look*. Hillsdale, NJ: The Analytic Press.

Gorkin, M. (1987) *The Uses of Countertransference*, Northvale, NJ: Aronson.

Greenberg, J. R. & Mitchell, S. A. (1983) *Object Relations in Psychoanalytic Theory*. Cambridge, MA: Harvard University Press.

Greenson, R. R. (1960) Empathy and its vicissitudes. *International Journal of Psycho-Analysis*, 41:418–424.

——— (1974) Loving, hating, and indifference towards the patient. *International Review of Psychoanalysis*, 1:259–266.

Grinberg, L. (1962) On a specific aspect of countertransference due to the patient's projective identification. *International Journal of Psycho-Analysis*, 31:81–84.

Grotstein, J. S. (1981) *Splitting and Projective Identification*. New York: Aronson.

Guntrip, H. (1971) *Psychoanalytic Theory, Therapy, and the Self*. New York: Basic Books.

Heimann, P. (1950) On countertransference. *International Journal of Psycho-Analysis*, 31:81–84.
Hendrick, I. (1950) *Facts and Theories of Psychoanalysis*. New York: Knopf.
Hoffman, I. (1983) The patient as interpreter of the analyst's experience. *Contemporary Psychoanalysis*, 19:389–422.
Isaacs, S. (1939) Criteria for interpretation. *International Journal of Psycho-Analysis*, 20:148–160.
Jaffee, D. S. (1968) The mechanism of projection: Its dual role in object relations. *International Journal of Psycho-Analysis*, 49:662–676.
Kernberg, O. (1965) Notes on countertransference. *Journal of the American Psychoanalytic Association*, 13:38–56.
——— (1975) *Borderline Conditions and Pathological Narcissism*. New York: Aronson.
——— (1976) *Object Relations Theory and Clinical Psychoanalysis*. New York: Aronson.
——— Burstein, E., Coyne, L., Appelbaum, A., Horwitz, L. & Voth, H. (1972) Psychotherapy and psychoanalysis: Final report of the Menninger Foundation's Psychotherapy Research Project. *Bulletin of the Menninger Clinic*, 36:1–275.
Klein, M. (1946) Notes on some schizoid mechanisms. *International Journal of Psycho-Analysis*, 33:433–438.
——— (1955) On identification. In: *Envy and Gratitude and Other Works, 1945–1963*. New York: Delacortte Press, 1975, pp. 141–175.
Kohut, H. (1959) Introspection, empathy, and psychoanalysis. An examination of the relationship between mode of observation and theory. *Journal of the American Psychoanalytic Association*, 7:459–483.
——— (1968) The psychoanalytic treatment of narcissistic personality disorders. *The Psychoanalytic Study of the Child*, 23:86–113. New York: International Universities Press.
——— (1971) *The Analysis of the Self*. New York: International Universities Press.
——— (1977) *The Restoration of the Self*. New York: International Universities Press.
Kris, E. (1952) *Psychoanalytic Explorations in Art*. New York: International Universities Press.
Kubie, L. (1952) Problems and techniques in psychoanalytic validation and progress. In: *Psychoanalysis as Science*, ed. E. Pumpian-Mindlin. Stanford, CA: Stanford University Press, pp. 74–89.
Lakovics, M. (1983) Classification of countertransference for utilization in supervision. *American Journal of Psychotherapy*, 37:245–257.

Langs, R. (1975) Therapeutic misalliances. *International Journal of Psychoanalytic Psychotherapy*, 4:77–105.
———. (1976) *The Therapeutic Interaction: Volume II*. New York: Aronson.
——— (1978) *Technique in Transition*, New York: Aronson.
——— (1982) *Psychotherapy, A Basic Text*. New York: Aronson.
Liberman, D. (1978) Affective response of the analyst to the patient's communications. *International Journal of Psycho-Analysis*, 59:335–340.
Little, M. (1951) Countertransference and the patient's response to it. *International Journal of Psycho-Analysis*, 32:32–40.
Little, M. (1957) "R"—The analyst's total response to his patient's needs. *International Journal of Psycho-Analysis*, 38:240–254.
Malin, A. & Grotstein, J. S. (1966) Projective identification in the therapeutic process. *International Journal of Psycho-Analysis*, 42:26–31.
Meissner, W. W. (1972) Notes on identification III. The concept of identification. *Psychoanalytic Quarterly*, 41:224–260.
——— (1980) A note on projective identification. *Journal of the American Psychoanalytic Association*, 28:43–67.
——— (1982) Notes on countertransference in borderline conditions. *International Journal of Psychoanalytic Psychotherapy*, 10:89–123.
Mintz, J., Luborsky, L. & Auerback. A. H. (1971) Dimensions of psychotherapy: A factor analytic study of ratings of psychotherapy sessions. *Journal of Consulting and Clinical Psychology*, 36:106–120.
Ogden, T. G. (1979) On projective identification. *International Journal of Psycho-Analysis*, 60:357–373.
——— (1982) *Projective Identification and Psychotherapeutic Technique*. New York: Aronson.
——— (1985) On potential space. *International Journal of Psycho-Analysis* 66:129–141.
Olinick, S. (1969) On empathy and regression in service of the other. *British Journal of Medical Psychology*, 42:41–49.
——— Poland, W. S., Grigg, K. A. & Granatir, W. L. (1973) The psychoanalytic work ego: Process and interpretation. *International Journal of Psycho-Analysis*, 54:143–151.
Racker, H. (1953) A contribution to the problem of countertransference. *International Journal of Psycho-Analysis*, 34:313–324.
——— (1957) The meanings and uses of countertransference. *Psychoanalytic Quarterly*, 26:303–357.
——— (1968) *Transference and Countertransference*. New York: International Universities Press.

Reich, A. (1951) On counter-transference. *International Journal of Psycho-Analysis*, 32:25–31.

——— (1960) Further remarks on countertransference. *International Journal of Psycho-Analysis*, 41:389–395.

——— (1966) *Psychoanalytic Contributions*. New York: International Universities Press.

Reik, T. (1937) *Surprise and the Psychoanalyst*. New York: Dutton.

——— (1948) *Listening with the Third Ear.* New York: Farrar, Strauss, & Young.

Ricoeur, P. (1977) The question of proof in Freud's psychoanalytic writings. *Journal of the American Psychoanalytic Association*, 25:835–871.

Roland, A. (1981) Induced emotional reactions and attitudes in the psychoanalyst as transference in actuality. *Psychoanalytic Review*, 68:45–74.

Rychlak, J. (1968) *A Philosophy of Science for Personality Theory.* New York: Rieger.

Sandler, J. (1976) Countertransference and role-responsiveness. *International Review of Psycho-Analysis*, 3:43–47.

Sandler, J. (1987) *Projection, Identification, Projective Identification.* Madison, CT: International Universities Press.

——— & Rosenblatt, B. (1962) The concept of the representational world. *The Psychoanalytic Study of the Child*, 17:128–145. New York: International Universities Press.

Schafer, R. (1954) *Psychoanalytic Interpretation in Rorschach Testing*. New York: Grune & Stratton.

——— (1959) Generative empathy in the treatment situation. *Psychoanalytic Quarterly*, 28:347–373.

——— (1968) *Aspects of Internalization*. New York: International Universities Press.

——— (1980) Narration in the psychoanalytic dialogue. *Critical Inquiry*, 7:29–53.

——— (1983) *The Analytic Attitude*. New York: Basic Books.

——— (1984) The pursuit of failure and the idealization of unhappiness. *American Psychologist*, 39:398–405.

Searles, H. F. (1965) *Collected Papers on Schizophrenia and Related Topics*. New York: International Universities Press.

——— (1975) The patient as therapist to his analyst. In: *Tactics and Techniques of Psychoanalytic Therapy. Vol. II*, ed. P. Giovachini. New York: Aronson, pp. 95–151.

Segal, H. (1964) *Introduction to the Work of Melanie Klein*. New York: Basic Books.

Shapiro, T. (1974) The development and distortions in empathy. *Psychoanalytic Quarterly*, 43:4–25.

Simmel, E. (1926) The "Doctor Game," illness and the profession of medicine. *International Journal of Psycho-Analysis*, 4:470–483.

Singer, B. & Luborsky, L. (1978) Countertransference: The status of clinical vs. quantitative research. In: *Effective Psychotherapy: A Handbook of Research*, ed. A. Gurman & A. Razin. New York: Pergamon.

Spence, D. P. (1982) *Narrative Truth and Historical Truth*. New York: Norton.

Stekel, W. (1911) *Die Sprache des Traumes*. Wiesbaden: 1922.

Sullivan, H. S. (1930) Socio-psychiatric research. *Schizophrenia as a Human Process*. New York: Norton, 1962.

——— (1931) The modified psychoanalytic treatment of schizophrenia. *Schizophrenia as a Human Process*. New York: Norton, 1962.

——— (1936) A note on the implications of psychiatry on the study of interpersonal relations for investigators in the social sciences. *The Fusion of Psychiatry and Social Science*. New York: Norton, 1964.

——— (1938) The data of psychiatry. *The Fusion of Psychiatry and Social Science*. New York: Norton, 1964.

——— (1940) *Concepts of Modern Psychiatry*. New York: Norton.

——— (1953) *The Interpersonal Theory of Psychiatry*. New York: Norton.

Tansey, M. J. & Burke, W. F. (1985) Projective identification and the empathic process. *Contemporary Psychoanalysis*, 21:42–69.

Tauber, E. S. (1954) Exploring the therapeutic use of countertransference data. *Psychiatry*, 17:331–336.

Tower, L. E. (1956) Countertransference. *Journal of the American Psychoanalytic Association*, 4:224–255.

Winnicott, D. W. (1936) Appetite and emotional development. In: *Through Paediatrics to Psychoanalysis*. London: Hogarth Press, 1958.

——— (1945) Primitive emotional development. In: *Through Paediatrics to Psychoanalysis*. London: Hogarth Press, 1958.

——— (1949) Hate in the countertransference. *International Journal of Psycho-Analysis*, 30:69–75.

——— (1960) The theory of the parent-infant relationship. *The Maturational Processes and the Facilitating Environment*. New York: International Universities Press, 1965.

——— (1965) *The Maturational Processes and the Facilitating Environment*. New York: International Universities Press.

——— (1971) The place where we live. In: *Playing and Reality.* New York: Basic Books, 1971, pp. 104–110.

Wolf, E. (1980) On the developmental line of selfobject relations. In: *Advances In Self Psychology,* ed. A. Goldberg. New York: International Universities Press.

Zetzel, E. R. (1965) Depression and the capacity to bear it. In: *Drives, Affects, and Behavior,* Vol. 2, ed. M. Schur. New York: International Universities Press.

Author Index

S

T

V

W

Z

Subject Index

U

V

W